# The HOLY FIRE of ECK

# Also by Harold Klemp

Animals Are Soul Too!
The Art of Spiritual Dreaming
Ask the Master, Books 1 and 2
Autobiography of a Modern Prophet
Be the HU: How to Become a Co-worker with God
Child in the Wilderness
A Cosmic Sea of Words: The ECKANKAR Lexicon
ECK Arahata Book
ECK Masters and You: An Illustrated Guide
ECK Wisdom Temples, Spiritual Cities, & Guides: A Brief History
Handbook for ECK Leaders
The Holy Fire of ECK, Books 1 and 2
Is Life a Random Walk?
Karmabusters
The Living Word, Books 1, 2, and 3
A Modern Prophet Answers Your Key Questions about Life
Past Lives, Dreams, and Soul Travel
Riding for the ECK Brand
Soul Travelers of the Far Country
The Spiritual Exercises of ECK
The Spiritual Laws of Life
The Temple of ECK
Those Wonderful ECK Masters
Welcome to the Wonderful World of ECK! Your Membership Guidebook
The Wind of Change
Wisdom from the Master on Spiritual Leadership: ECK Leader's Guide
Wisdom of the Heart, Books 1 and 2
Workbook for Be the HU
Workbook for Wisdom from the Master on Spiritual Leadership
Your Road Map to the ECK Teachings: ECKANKAR Study Guide, Volumes 1 and 2
Youth Ask a Modern Prophet about Life, Love, and God

**The Immortality of Soul Series**
The Awakened Heart
The Language of Soul
Love—The Keystone of Life
Touching the Face of God
Truth Has No Secrets

**The Mahanta Transcripts Series**
Journey of Soul, Book 1
How to Find God, Book 2
The Secret Teachings, Book 3
The Golden Heart, Book 4
Cloak of Consciousness, Book 5
Unlocking the Puzzle Box, Book 6
The Eternal Dreamer, Book 7
The Dream Master, Book 8
We Come as Eagles, Book 9
The Drumbeat of Time, Book 10
What Is Spiritual Freedom? Book 11
How the Inner Master Works, Book 12
The Slow Burning Love of God, Book 13
The Secret of Love, Book 14
Our Spiritual Wake-Up Calls, Book 15
How to Survive Spiritually in Our Times, Book 16

**Spiritual Wisdom Series**
Spiritual Wisdom on Conquering Fear
Spiritual Wisdom on Health and Healing
Spiritual Wisdom on Prayer, Meditation, and Contemplation
Spiritual Wisdom on Relationships

**Stories to Help You See God in Your Life**
The Book of ECK Parables, Volumes 1, 2, and 3
Stories to Help You See God in Your Life, ECK Parables, Book 4

**Workbooks for Discourses**
Workbook for the Easy Way Discourses
Workbook for the ECK Dream 1 Discourses
Workbook for the Master 3 Discourses
Workbook for the Master 4 Discourses

This book has been authored by and published under the supervision of the Mahanta, the Living ECK Master, Sri Harold Klemp. It is the Word of ECK.

# The HOLY FIRE of ECK

Book 3

Harold Klemp

ECKANKAR
Minneapolis
www.Eckankar.org

**The Holy Fire of ECK,** Book 3

Copyright © 2009 ECKANKAR

All rights reserved. No part of this book may be reproduced, stored in a retrieval system, or transmitted in any form by any means, whether electronic, mechanical, photocopying, recording, or otherwise, without prior written permission of ECKANKAR.

The terms ECKANKAR, ECK, EK, MAHANTA, SOUL TRAVEL, and VAIRAGI, among others, are trademarks of ECKANKAR, PO Box 2000, Chanhassen, MN 55317-2000 USA. 070530

Printed in USA
Library of Congress Control Number: 2008929266
ISBN: 978-1-57043-255-2

Compiled by Mary Carroll Moore
Edited by Patrick Carroll, Joan Klemp, and Anthony Moore

Text illustrations by Ann Hubert
Author photo by Robert Huntley

∞ This paper meets the requirements of ANSI/NISO Z39.48-1992 (Permanence of Paper).

# Contents

**Introduction** .................................... ix

**Chapter One: Walking Your Own Path to God**
1. The Waltz of the Wind ......................... 3
2. Your Own Path to God......................... 7
3. No Normal People ............................ 11
4. More Things in Heaven and Earth.............. 17

**Chapter Two: Daily Spiritual Disciplines**
5. Getting Back to the Basics of Life .............. 25
6. Why We Contemplate and Don't Meditate ...... 29
7. The Name of the Game ....................... 35

**Chapter Three: The Mahanta's Love for You**
8. The Cage of Life.............................. 43
9. No Charge ................................... 49
10. The Master's Enchanting Love ................. 53

**Chapter Four: How to Be a Better Vehicle for ECK**
11. A Change in Consciousness—Not an Overnight Event ....................................... 61
12. War, Peace, and the Task of ECKANKAR ....... 65
13. Bring In the Candles ......................... 71

**Chapter Five: Tests and Challenges of the Higher Initiate**
14. Nothing Succeeds like Failure.................. 79
15. Look for the Gifts! ........................... 85

16. A Pot of Gold or Something Greater? . . . . . . . . . . . 89
17. In God's Time . . . . . . . . . . . . . . . . . . . . . . . . . . . . . . 93

## Chapter Six: Overcoming Illusion
18. Home Is Where the Heart Is . . . . . . . . . . . . . . . . . . 101
19. The Gift of the Eternal Teachings . . . . . . . . . . . . . . 105
20. What Kind of Experience Leads to God? . . . . . . . 111
21. The Golden Ring of Truth . . . . . . . . . . . . . . . . . . . 117

## Chapter Seven: Living in Service to All Life
22. How the Holy Spirit Helps You . . . . . . . . . . . . . . . 125
23. The Long Arm of the Mahanta . . . . . . . . . . . . . . . . 131
24. Meetings with Two ECK Masters . . . . . . . . . . . . . . 135

## Chapter Eight: Creating a Life of Love and Beauty
25. A Window-Washing Miracle . . . . . . . . . . . . . . . . . 143
26. No Security Here, but Where? . . . . . . . . . . . . . . . . 149
27. Gratitude Shows You Can Love . . . . . . . . . . . . . . . 155
28. It's a Good Life. . . . . . . . . . . . . . . . . . . . . . . . . . . . . 159

## Chapter Nine: A New Threshold of Love
29. No Greater Love . . . . . . . . . . . . . . . . . . . . . . . . . . . 167
30. What Gift Would You Give to the ECK Masters? . . . . . . . . . . . . . . . . . . . . . . . . . . . . . . . . . . 173
31. The Nature of the ECK Initiations . . . . . . . . . . . . . 177
32. God's Searing Love . . . . . . . . . . . . . . . . . . . . . . . . . 183
33. Closer to Finding God . . . . . . . . . . . . . . . . . . . . . . 187

**Bibliography** . . . . . . . . . . . . . . . . . . . . . . . . . . . . . . . . 191

**About the Author**. . . . . . . . . . . . . . . . . . . . . . . . . . . . 195

Sri Harold Klemp, the Mahanta, the Living ECK Master shows you that the path of ECK has no limits for those who are willing to listen to the Mahanta and follow their hearts.

# Introduction

Often when we make our plans, the winds can change things. Looking from the human state of consciousness, we're looking from the toes. So we try to look from a higher viewpoint.

We're looking for happiness, contentment, no matter how many winds are blowing. No matter how life beats on us.

But we're really looking for something greater—for spiritual freedom. The ecstasy of drinking from the cup of the Holy Spirit, the nectar of SUGMAD.

It brings ecstasy, and you can enjoy it, but at some point you have to come back to earth and pick up the pieces around you.

We live in the ecstasy of divine love but come back here to bring harmony about us—to see sunshine when others see storm. And that is what is difficult here.

What is spirituality? It's very simple. But in playing out, it's complicated. We need to put our emotions aside and say, Let my world be harmonious and peaceful and beautiful.

This is where the Spiritual Exercises of ECK come in handy. Even a quick stand-up exercise to ask the Master for help when it's needed. This is one of the functions of the Mahanta, the Living ECK Master.

The spiritual exercises are so important because they purify us, uplift us.

If you knew nothing about ECK but a spiritual exercise, you would have all you need if you did it with love. You would get it all.

How do you speak about beingness? Encouraging someone to *just be* is nice, but it doesn't just happen.

The Mahanta, the Living ECK Master can lay out a plan—and it's a good plan—but he can't make someone follow the path or follow the plan. We're talking about free will.

Spiritually in ECK it's very simple: Do the Spiritual Exercises of ECK with love, and keep your face to the Mahanta, the Living ECK Master.

In these, my quarterly messages to you in the *H.I. Letter*, I offer you the cup. But it is up to you to drink the nectar of God.

The way to God is like a walk on an early summer morning in a meadow, garden, or park. Fresh and alive.

## Chapter One

# Walking Your Own Path to God

# 1
# The Waltz of the Wind

*If* memory serves me, "the waltz of the wind" is a phrase from a country-and-western song I've heard sung by the legendary Hank Williams.

"The waltz of the wind" is also an apt metaphor for the action of the ECK, the Life Current, the Holy Spirit, the Voice of God.

Let us reflect upon that for a few moments.

The seeker in *Stranger by the River*, by Paul Twitchell, was at the end of his wits. He'd come a long way, though. For one thing, "He no longer drifted with the tide of mankind which moved through the world like logs at the mercy of the storm on the river's surface."

He sat quietly on a bank of the great river that flowed from the mighty Himalayas. He could have likened the water to the river of God, which is forever flowing from the heart of God.

It flows into all the worlds below, through all of creation. It flows outward.

But then, very unlike the great earthly river, It reverses course. The awesome Life Stream flows back through creation and once more into the heart of God, the Ocean of Love and Mercy.

> *"The waltz of the wind" is an apt metaphor for the action of the ECK, the Life Current, the Holy Spirit, the Voice of God.*

The seeker knew some of this. But only a true Master could impart the deep secrets of God.

And then he saw him—his Master, the wonderful ECK Master Rebazar Tarzs. Now the seeker's journey back home to God could begin in earnest.

In time, the seeker would learn more about the action of the Spirit of God. It is indeed very much like the waltz of the wind, coming and going by some unseen law, even as the steps of a waltz follow a pattern of moving rhythmically, smoothly, and gracefully here and there.

Yes, he would learn more, even as you did.

And your first, halting steps in ECK stumbled upon things about It you would never once have dreamed. You found, for example, that the ECK could be seen, actually seen, as a light of some color like pink, orange, blue, violet, yellow, or white.

It was visible; what a revelation! But did it ever occur to you there might be another side to that glorious Life Stream?

Sooner or later, you learned that "the Audible Sound Current" spoke of that other side. The Voice of God could be heard—yes, actually heard—as clearly as any number of ordinary and not-so-ordinary sounds. Maybe It was like a passing train, or a rushing wind.

Remember? Of course, you do.

In time, you learned another secret: the Voice of God was also the bringer and giver of God's love. This boundless love gave meaning and fulfillment to your life. Also peace and understanding. You began to understand who and what your neighbors were and did.

*This boundless love gave meaning and fulfillment to your life. Also peace and understanding.*

Good behavior, bad behavior, and every shade of behavior in between are but reflections of the amount of God's love in each Soul, larger or smaller. And so, you learned how to dance with the good ones and steer clear of the rest.

You have thus, since your first wobbly steps on the dance floor of ECK, learned the waltz of the wind.

Let It guide you to bring Its sweet breath to seekers you meet on your journey.

*Let It guide you to bring Its sweet breath to seekers you meet on your journey.*

# 2
# Your Own Path to God

𝒴ou are on your own path to God. The Mahanta, the Living ECK Master, with your permission, leads you from the stagnation of the human mind and lifts you into the pure worlds of God's love and truth.

And there you stay, if you remain steadfast in the holy Light and Sound. The imperishable worlds.

"This is the key to the spiritual worlds," says Paul Twitchell in *The Spiritual Notebook*. "We must surrender to the ECK, and It will give us everything in life."

New members of ECK offer thanks for the gift of the ECK teachings. The people are vibrant, alive to the love and grace that abounds upon their own path to God. The way to God is like a walk on an early summer morning in a meadow, garden, or park. Fresh and alive. A joyful state of wonder—and yes, bliss.

\* \* \*

A recent member from England tells of his gratitude for the gift of love he's found on his own path in ECK.

*You are on your own path to God.*

"I would first like to thank Harold, the Living ECK Master, the Mahanta for all his help on the inner planes during the past few months. I feel that events are beginning to work out and my reaction to them is much less anxious. Even when they seem to have hurt attached to them, it feels that I can embrace that feeling and begin to walk through it with more confidence now."

\* \* \*

People sometimes make loud complaints about an uneven playing field. They mean to say, "I would have won the game if the odds had not been stacked against me."

What an excuse.

Life *is* an even playing field. However, the players who arrive for the big game are unequal in skill and desire. Why blame the field?

After all, why blame anyone, least of all themselves? People *want* to be unequal. They want to be an expert in a chosen field, a champion, or a noted authority. It's a part of their own path to God, this striving for excellence.

Leaders who try to misshape the game of life in a bold attempt to render all people equal in wealth, for example, face bitter disappointment, because people will never be equal in material goods. Only as Soul.

Each person brings a unique set of virtues or defects to the game.

The virtues, gained over many lifetimes, reveal such things as love, charity, and wisdom. These people are the enlightened ones. They have gained a better understanding of their true role in life.

*Life* is *an even playing field. However, the players who arrive for the big game are unequal in skill and desire.*

Defects include lying, cheating, the misuse of power to get one's way, greed, and lust. These are among the most destructive of passions.

People advertise who they are by the leaders they choose to speak and act on their behalf.

"The love of liberty is the love of others," said William Hazlitt, an essayist of the nineteenth century. "The love of power is the love of ourselves."

These two motivators compel the actions of every human being to one degree or another. It's a choice between the left or the right fork in the road. The left fork is the route to mental confusion, while the right fork is the direct path to God, the way of ECK. The left one offers illusion and false hopes. The right one sees the development of vision and true service.

A great deal of cleansing takes place in the normal run of life to attain spiritual maturity.

A newcomer to ECK told the following story about the Blue Light, a sign of the Master's presence. Let's call her Judy.

Judy had attended the ECK Worship Services in her town for two years. The place of worship had a Blue Star on display, and Judy's heart opened each time at the sight of it. She fell in love with that shade of blue.

In fact, her love for that color carried over to work. Judy, then employed in a jewelry store, developed a fascination for some blue stones that reminded her of the Blue Star. These stones happened to be ice sapphires. She put them on layaway.

When she got the sapphires out of layaway, she found some tiny diamonds to go around the

*It's a choice between the left or the right fork in the road. The right one sees the development of vision and true service.*

blue sapphires. She put these diamonds on layaway too.

Later, when she retrieved the diamonds, she had the blue sapphires set in a ring, surrounded by the tiny diamonds. A short time after bringing the ring home, a violent incident happened to her in the parking lot of a grocery store.

Two women at a nearby car had asked her help, so Judy went over. The violent one ripped her purse from her wrist and threatened her life.

She flung Judy into their car. The lower half of Judy's body was hanging out of the car as the car dragged her across the pavement. She fell under the car. The rear wheel rolled toward her face, but in that instant she chose to live.

A man's voice took over. "No!" it commanded as the tire jolted closer. Something very soft rolled over her, and the wheel missed her. (It was the Mahanta who'd spoken.)

Flat on the pavement, she saw her arm bathed in a beautiful blue light. It was from the ring on her hand, yet from outside herself. A blue color like the Blue Star of ECK.

The police came. She gave them a license-plate number. The driver got two years in prison; the violent one got away.

But Judy had seen the Master's love and protection. The Blue Star and the Master were one.

For many years, you, the Higher Initiate of ECK, have been on this right fork to God. Review *The Spiritual Notebook* to renew the freshness of Soul's walk on God's early summer morn.

You are on your own path to God. Walk it true.

---

*For many years, you, the Higher Initiate of ECK, have been on this right fork to God. Review* The Spiritual Notebook *to renew the freshness of Soul's walk on God's early summer morn.*

# 3
# No Normal People

*I*n an ECK office survey, chelas asked for very specific help. These three topics were at the top of the list:
- How to surrender to avoid needless suffering?
- How to enliven their spiritual exercises?
- How to know that the ECK (Holy Spirit) is working in their lives?

*How to surrender to avoid needless suffering?*

As the staff person who took the survey noted, "These topics are addressed in the first few articles of *Be the HU*." But I'd like to add some thoughts.

Joan went to the post office to conduct some business. The three regular postal clerks were on vacation, and three fill-ins were in place. Joan asked one clerk, a surly man who'd served her some weeks earlier as a fill-in, to please check if she had a package. He threw back a dark look.

"I'll need to see some identification."

Joan returned a puzzled look. Show an ID for a package that might not be there?

With all the self-importance of an uncivil servant, he said, "There are no normal people here today!" That explained everything. It'd been a hard day all around.

The difference between them is that the clerk holds on to things he feels are out of order, while Joan lets the slights of other people go. She doesn't hang on to a bad encounter with a person who behaves in a boorish manner. She surrenders to the ECK. The Golden-tongued Wisdom had spoken in the clerk's own words: "There are no normal people here today." He'd then said he couldn't issue a postal money order—a basic post-office service.

Joan, of course, persisted. Another clerk was happy to sell her a money order.

Let the ECK, or the Mahanta, help carry your frustrations. It's the key to happiness. But how to accomplish that? The discipline of remembering to surrender is part of one's spiritual discipline. Yes, this sounds like no answer at all, but it's the individual's responsibility to remember. That's what consciousness is for.

Let's add, too, that the postal clerk's idea of service to people goes begging. It's not an example for an ECKist.

Service in ECK means being an agent for the Mahanta. It requires respect for others.

The Holy ECK feeds all with the bread and waters of life. So how could a spiritually alert person do less than serve It with love and humility? This attitude should be like a shining light to the world. True love and humility show in all one's dealings. Build and support people.

An old saying has it: "Whose bread I eat, his song I sing."

*Let the ECK, or the Mahanta, help carry your frustrations. It's the key to happiness.*

Wouldn't a loving and humble ECKist recognize the ECK and the Mahanta as the source of his very subsistence? Then how could he ever serve the Kal, the negative force?

Back to the ECK survey.

Some chelas wanted to know how to tell that the ECK was working in their lives.

If someone takes Its blessings for granted, habit will have shut his eyes to the everyday miracles of the Holy Spirit in evidence in all areas of his life. He could observe the lives of other chelas. These ECK writings are full of their stories. However, his eyes must be open.

It's the old catch-22.

A newcomer to ECKANKAR first saw pictures of ECK Masters in 1979. That was the end of her connection with ECKANKAR until a short time ago, when she called the ECK office to ask for information.

She reported that back in 1979 she recognized all the ECK Masters in the portraits on display at an ECK center. An ECKist said they'd been dead for centuries. The shock was too great. She ran from the place screaming.

Yet a lot of living had taken place since 1979. Now, she asked for books about the ECK Masters, because several had come to teach over the years in the dream state. She counted Rebazar Tarzs, Lai Tsi, and Gopal Das among her illustrious teachers.

The ECK was surely in her life.

How to tell when the ECK is at work in your life? Open your eyes! Look around. The evidence is there. Learn from the experiences of others;

*How to tell when the ECK is at work in your life? Open your eyes! Look around. The evidence is there.*

recognize your own as you used to do. There's no easy way in that regard. Your state of awareness is up to you.

The third concern that chelas expressed on the survey was how to enliven their spiritual exercises.

Here, too, there's a connection between your inner and outer lives. When you're solid with the Mahanta, the Living ECK Master, other ECK chelas will know. The Light and Sound of God permeate your very being—or they do not. No one can fake that. And guess what? This connection starts at the foundation: the Spiritual Exercises of ECK.

Others can "read" you. They can tell your inner state by your words and deeds. These must agree with the teachings of ECK.

Someone once observed that the reason church members need so much reassurance is because of the pastor's own shallow faith. In consequence, the parishioners were unable to minister to newcomers. So, an ECK leader must examine the evidence of his own faith to learn why there are so few who come to ECKANKAR in his own area.

It boils down to this: Are you willing to put the Mahanta first in your life? Then those who are ready for the way of God's Light and Sound will find you. Again, do your spiritual exercises.

One High Initiate experiments with new spiritual exercises, and you may wish to try her discovery of how to have a spiritual healing. She sees each of her five bodies fanned out in a row. A shower of white light from God streams down, cleansing and purifying her bodies on all levels.

*The Light and Sound of God permeate your very being—or they do not. Others can "read" you. They can tell your inner state by your words and deeds.*

Note the divine Sound too.

Focus on the five bodies for a minute or two. Then surrender to the Light and Sound as they wash over you, and let go of all useless mental and emotional baggage.

*Surrender to the Light and Sound as they wash over you.*

That will leave only *superior* normal people among the true followers of ECK.

# 4
# More Things in Heaven and Earth

"*There are more things in heaven and earth, Horatio, / Than are dreamt of in your philosophy.*"

Many have heard this famous quotation from Shakespeare's *Hamlet*. Few would be so brazen as to say they number among the sages who know more about the mysteries than Joe and Jane across the street, yet most act that way. Let someone offer a view of religion or philosophy that differs in the smallest degree from their own beliefs, then watch the sparks fly.

So, in practice, lip service and hand service of a kind belong to the sages. The multitudes, barring a scattering of saints, suffer the spiritual condition of their hands not knowing the utterances of their keeper's lips. And vice versa.

Why, do you suppose, do sages hold the cards of truth and knowledge so close to their chests?

It's in the interest of self-protection.

A sage like an ECK Master will not throw pearls before the swine, because they may turn on him. What use has a hog for precious stones? His god is his belly.

*The multitudes suffer the spiritual condition of their hands not knowing the utterances of their keeper's lips. And vice versa.*

Truth, however, is freely available. It is all around us, but couched in clothing of a different kind. So we laugh and cry with the joys and sorrows of a fictional bird like Jonathan Livingston Seagull, but don't dare let anyone say that Soul resides in some bird feathers.

That would provoke an occasion of a "tar and feather" party.

Of course, churches, political parties, social groups, and families do have the right to admit to their circles only kindred spirits. Imagine a stranger showing up at a family Christmas gathering and making himself right at home. He helps himself to the buffet, the drinks, and makes free to join in the conversation.

That would take brass. How could he expect else than to land in a snowbank outside the front door, propelled there by a couple of family mehearties (stout fellows)?

So a church may welcome visitors. However, unless the clergy has sold out the group's beliefs or is in desperate need of members, the sacraments will be denied guests. Who would expect something other?

In ECKANKAR, too, there are programs for the public palate as well as those for ECKists alone.

Initiations are an example of a rite reserved for ECK members. Each initiation, in turn, is only available to individuals who've passed certain tests. So the initiates in a given circle share a common bond. Divine knowledge is like a pool of refreshing water that one may use to clean up in

*Divine knowledge is like a pool of refreshing water. Depending on what use each makes of the opportunity to bathe in these Waters of Life, he will gain in love, wisdom, and understanding.*

and enjoy. Depending on what use each makes of the opportunity to bathe in these Waters of Life, he will gain in love, wisdom, and understanding.

Since each Soul is a unique creation with individual goals, It differs from all others in even that circle of initiation.

With this basic unique character behind the creation of each individual, is it any wonder that a range of ideas and understandings should be found even among, say, the initiates of the Fifth Circle?

That's all well. However, if the behavior of someone falls outside the borders of the Fifth, he is ready for a change. Easy, there. All change need not be in an upward direction. There is down too.

Change may also include standing still. All is relative. If the others in the Fifth Circle, for example, move on to the Sixth but one stays behind—that's change of a static sort.

Now here's the secret: it doesn't matter. Soul, remember, is a unique creation of God. It's right where It is. All's OK.

Spiritual unfoldment is not a race between the hare and tortoise. Where are the winners and losers? Such a dichotomy has no existence in the true spiritual planes that begin at the Soul Plane. There, all is one.

All is one in a way that bedevils human understanding. For example, gays will no longer be gay. But then again, heterosexuals will no more be heterosexuals either. In a talk once I mentioned the first half of the equation above but neglected the second part. That gained the wrath of narrow-

*Soul is a unique creation of God. It's right where It is. All's OK. Spiritual unfoldment is not a race between the hare and tortoise.*

minded gays and the triumphant joy of narrow-minded heterosexuals.

Each had the idea of there being some exclusion from the true spiritual worlds unless changes were forthcoming.

Again, what difference does sexual preference make? We are judged by society's laws of morality and must abide by them or suffer. These laws keep order. It's the rule of the Kal, or negative, worlds.

But spiritual laws are not those of society. In all cases, they are of a higher order. They offer love, wisdom, freedom, and understanding to all that are of the consciousness to accept them.

However, the starting point for getting spiritual freedom is in giving it to others.

Our freedom stops where our neighbor's begins.

If I were to speak of the limitless abilities of a Soul to run dozens of bodies at once in various worlds at the same time, it would cause some eyebrows to lift. They would lift on people who have trouble running their one human body. These people cannot imagine trying to oversee twelve different lives at once, because it's outside their range of consciousness.

It is people of limited consciousness who burn others at the stake, steal the property of their neighbor aided and abetted by faulty human law, hate, and the like.

Such individuals exist at every level of consciousness. Excepting, of course, those who live and move in the true spiritual realms of divine wisdom.

> *The starting point for getting spiritual freedom is in giving it to others.*

It is due to the imperfections of the many states of consciousness that "There are more things in heaven and earth, Horatio, / Than are dreamt of in your philosophy."

The name of the game is survival. But only in part. It is mainly about unfolding, reaching new levels of learning, understanding, and wisdom.

## Chapter Two

# Daily Spiritual Disciplines

# 5
# Getting Back to the Basics of Life

*Do* you remember Aesop's fable about Hercules, a mythical Greek hero known for his strength, and the wagoner?

A wagoner once drove a heavy load along a very muddy road. The horses pulled for all they were worth, but, no doubt about it, the wagon was stuck. The wagoner laid his whip to the horses without effect. But he disdained to get off and put his own shoulder to a wheel. Therefore, the wagon remained firmly mired in the mud. As a last resort, he prayed to Hercules the Strong for assistance.

Hercules duly appeared. "Listen," he snapped, "get off and put your *own* shoulder to the wheel!"

That was one way of getting back to the basics of life. But there is another. The wagoner wanted Hercules to do the hard work, without lifting a finger to get out of his own mire. An ECKist, on the other hand, does absolutely all he can to remove himself from a difficulty, but then he takes the additional step of asking for the Mahanta's aid.

*An ECKist does all he can to remove himself from a difficulty, but then he takes the additional step of asking for the Mahanta's aid.*

25

It's the best way of getting back to the basics of life.

I addressed this very same theme in a recent article to the RESAs, but at a higher spiritual level. You will profit greatly if you take it to heart. It reads:

People can test the very limits of your patience. And so often they do. That robs you of whatever peace and contentment you thought you had once gained.

So how do you get back to the basics of life? Go back to the big picture.

In *The Shariyat-Ki-Sugmad*, Book Two, it says: "If a chela of ECK can have no peace within himself, it is written that he cannot bring peace to others. The mystery of peace is found only within one, and he has to distribute his state of selflessness to others to bring degrees of peace; that is, if they are ready and willing to accept this quality of God within themselves."

Doesn't that evoke the very picture of Peddar Zaskq in *The Tiger's Fang* as he looks upon the warring worlds within him? Somehow, he had to learn to resolve that ruinous conflict within himself.

He did, and you can too.

Again, the *Shariyat*, Book Two, says this: "Those living in the state of selflessness will speak gently and carefully, selecting their words to give life to others."

Now, this can only happen when you are at peace within yourself.

Remember the words of ECK Master Rebazar

---

*The* Shariyat, Book Two, says this: "Those living in the state of selflessness will speak gently and carefully, selecting their words to give life to others."

Tarzs to the seeker in *Stranger by the River*.

"Before you can enter into the Kingdom of Heaven," he says, "it is necessary that you balance the scale of harmony within thyself."

So everything begins with peace. Without it, there is no selflessness. No reaching a true seeker. No dealing effectively with the many people you run across in your everyday duties and responsibilities.

It is vitally important for you to periodically make a careful assessment of yourself. Who are you? Where are you? What are your spiritual goals? Have they inadvertently slipped from the lofty standards you had once set for yourself? Lots of questions, these.

The *Shariyat*, Book Two, puts it all into perspective. It's a reminder about the power of the Spiritual Exercises of ECK. The stresses of daily living can cause us to forget.

It reads: "To the ordinary man the mantra would appear to be nonsensical, a sound which is only the response of the brain to a certain range of vibration transmitted by the air that surrounds him. But, nevertheless, it is a powerful instrument of love and detachment for that ECK chela who practices it regularly. He reaches out to people whom he will never know and changes the course of their lives from the Kal forces which might be gripping them to the ECK which will lead them to God."

There's a lot of wisdom here for you to get back to the basics of life.

---

*It is vitally important for you to periodically make a careful assessment of yourself. Who are you? Where are you? What are your spiritual goals? Have they slipped from the lofty standards you once set for yourself?*

# 6
# Why We Contemplate and Don't Meditate

A newer Higher Initiate recently raised a provocative question. He is a successful publisher of a magazine that features articles on spiritual matters. As such, he's helped seekers find ECKANKAR.

He wondered if more new people would find the teachings of ECK attractive if we used the word *meditation* for *contemplation*.

It is a compelling thought. But, in the end, it would not work as envisioned, because *meditation* would attract people who aren't ready for the ECK teachings. Those who meditate center upon the things of the mental world. And it is important that they do so. The Mental Plane is a finishing school in Soul's evolution, for Soul needs the experience of meditation. There is a lot that goes with that stage, from a spiritual viewpoint.

When a meditator has learned everything he can there, then he'll be ready to move on to the teachings of ECK. And he'll be attracted by a spiritual feature of the teachings that is quite apart from a cosmetic change like the use of *contemplation*

*The Mental Plane is a finishing school in Soul's evolution. When a meditator has learned everything he can there, then he'll be ready to move on to the teachings of ECK.*

instead of *meditation* in our public presentations.

I'd like to thank this brother for his suggestion. It is well taken. It shows he's open to trying new ideas to reach seekers. The ECKANKAR Spiritual Center welcomes such ideas and will evaluate them for possible use. So please keep them coming.

There are indeed many people who are ready for ECKANKAR. Their pre-ECK experiences are inspiring. Would you like to hear Ellen's story? (Her name is changed to protect her privacy.) It is one such experience.

Ellen was a sixteen-year-old student when she had her first encounter with the Sound and Light of ECK, the Holy Spirit. This was seven years before she became a member of ECKANKAR.

It was the night before the entrance accreditation for university study, and Ellen was a bundle of nerves. Passing the accreditation meant all the world to her, because it was a very desirable thing to get. Accreditation told which students did not have to sit the usual entrance exams. It looked at a student's grades through the year and thus determined who would be excused from taking the usual exams.

Ellen did poorly on exams, so a lot was riding on the entrance accreditation.

That night, she couldn't get to sleep. Her heart was pounding. She kept thinking, *What if I don't get it?* Some four or five hours she lay there, eyes wide open.

Then it happened.

Suddenly, Ellen was floating toward the bright-

> *There are indeed many people who are ready for ECKANKAR. Their pre-ECK experiences are inspiring.*

est light she'd ever seen. A feeling of bliss and happiness swept through her whole body. It was an experience beyond words. The light shone brighter and brighter until she vibrated with love from head to toe. Then she fell into a peaceful sleep.

Seven years later, all the pieces fell into place.

Ellen had been wondering, *Is ECKANKAR right for me?* So one night before going to sleep she asked for a sign. She got it. The Mahanta had heard and responded in a big way.

She awoke in the middle of the night to a tremendous sound, a sound so loud that she feared it was a plane about to crash through the roof. Her heart was pounding wildly.

*This is a very powerful sign*, she thought.

And so it surely was. It was, in fact, one of the many sounds with which SUGMAD (God) talks to us. The Sound is God's Voice, and It speaks volumes.

The next morning, Ellen sent for her membership in ECKANKAR and soon began to study the discourse lessons.

But there was more to come.

Just a short month later, while heading toward the polytechnic building on campus to attend a computer class, she encountered the Light of God. It appeared in a cheerful and buoyant way. The Inner Master was now giving her an experience with one of the manifestations of the divine light.

It was a delightful manifestation. This is how she first noticed it.

Ellen had happened to glance down at her feet.

> *Ellen had been wondering,* Is ECKANKAR right for me? *She awoke in the middle of the night to a tremendous sound, a sound so loud that she feared it was a plane about to crash through the roof. This is a very powerful sign, she thought.*

On both shoes was a circle of blue light, which remained in the center of each shoe. So the whole day long, she walked around campus with eyes looking down at the circles of light on her shoes, for she sensed they spoke of the Mahanta, the Inner Master. He was walking with her, every single step of the way.

\* \* \*

Why do we put so much attention on the Light and Sound in ECKANKAR? It is for a very good reason.

They convey the fullness of God's love to us.

This brings us back to *contemplation* versus *meditation*. Is there a difference? There surely is. In a sense, one who contemplates is like a feather riding the wind, while one who meditates is much like a dry leaf fallen to the ground.

Meditation has its limits. Its domain reaches only to the mental realm. But contemplation can rise higher, to the Soul Plane and well beyond, into the highest states of consciousness.

So words do matter.

One who meditates is therefore not able to open to the full measure of God's love. But he doesn't know it. He's chosen the lesser of two ways of doing a spiritual exercise due to an unconscious fear of getting more divine love than he can possibly handle.

Jalal ad-Din ar-Rumi, the thirteenth-century poet and sage, was a disciple of ECK Master Shamus-i-Tabriz. Rumi once asked him, "Shams, why this inconsistency? That we live within love and yet we run away?"

A good question.

It's due to a state of consciousness still too young to accept a greater amount of divine love. So we run away.

Meditation is much like a drag chute deployed on a jet fighter landing on a short runway. The drag chute slows things down. It keeps things from going too far.

A meditator is guided to the right spiritual discipline, for it suits his state of consciousness. When he's ready for more divine love, he will learn the methods of contemplation.

Ellen contemplates. After the Mahanta, the Living ECK Master had given her the two experiences with the Sound and Light, she now contemplates. And she often hears God's Sound and sees the Light through her practice of the Spiritual Exercises of ECK.

Her story is a reminder to you of two things. There are people who are ready for the next step too. Would you help them find it? Also, remember to contemplate. It's the only way to go higher.

*There are people who are ready for the next step too. Would you help them find it? Also, remember to contemplate. It's the only way to go higher.*

# 7
# The Name of the Game

You well know some of the ways that life can shove you into a corner and squeeze you. It is tough love in all its glory. You feel like a lemon, then: squeezed until there's nothing left to give. All the acid is squeezed out.

Having survived this onslaught, you smile and pat yourself on the back. You have won again. After all, the name of the game is survival, isn't it?

Survival is part of the game for sure. But life's squeezings leave us sweeter somehow. Maybe they give us backbone. Maybe a code of honor. Maybe the ability to tell right from wrong—by our own lights, of course.

In other words, tough love, meted out by our no-nonsense tutor, Life, has installed a moral compass in us.

Let us look at an example of that.

Clarence Thomas is one of nine justices on the United States Supreme Court. Long before he gained that lofty position, he was a cash-strapped young lawyer trying to feed his family.

One day, on his way to work, he spotted a

*Life's squeezings leave us sweeter somehow. Maybe they give us backbone. Maybe a code of honor. Maybe the ability to tell right from wrong—by our own lights, of course.*

wallet on the sidewalk. He began to count the bills. At six hundred dollars, he stopped counting; there were more. The owner's name was inside, so Thomas called him. A gruff voice answered. Later, the owner arrived at his office to claim the wallet. Suspiciously, he began to count the bills.

"It's all there!" Thomas said, peeved.

The man peeled a five-dollar bill from the stack of bills and held it out. Thomas snapped, "I didn't do it for the money!" The man walked out without even a word of thanks.

This story tells of a principled young man whose destiny was to lead him to a cherished seat on the highest court in the land. He did need the money. Who would ever have known? No one! Yet he did the right thing, because *he* would have known.

In his memoir, *My Grandfather's Son*, he writes: "Honesty is what you do when no one is looking."

You have a destiny too. Yours is to become a Co-worker with God, an ECK Master in the Ancient Order of Vairagi Adepts. Even now, the Mahanta, the Living ECK Master is testing you. The course to Mastership is a go-at-your-own-speed one, with some version of a wallet-on-the-street test.

The name of the game, again, is survival. But only in part. In reality, it is much more than just survival. It is mainly about unfolding, reaching new levels of learning, understanding, and wisdom.

This brings to mind the example of the Knights Templars. They were members of a military-religious order in the Middle Ages and were also

*The course to Mastership is a go-at-your-own-speed one, with some version of a wallet-on-the-street test.*

known as the Poor Knights of Christ. In a word, they were the first knight-monks. Their duty was to protect pilgrims in the Holy Land.

One account has it that the nine founding members of the Knights Templars were, in fact, members of a secret order of European knights, the Order of Rebirth in Sion (Zion).

Of interest to us here is how they were chosen. The elders of this secret order would be on the lookout for the brightest, biggest, and smartest youths from a closely knit group of "friendly families." Most young boys were trained in the martial arts like swordplay, shooting arrows with bow and crossbow, running, riding, wrestling, and other activities.

Those the elders had their eye on received the same training as did all the other sons of the nobility, who nonetheless were not destined to become candidates for the secret order.

When a youth of one of these "friendly families" neared the age of maturity, around age eighteen, one or, usually, more of the secret elders would nominate him for membership in the secret order. Only one youth per generation would be considered in each family. And he could pass or fail.

This order was a highly select group of knights. When the elders met in conclave, they might determine that none of the candidates measured up to the order's strict criteria. In that case, all from that generation were passed over. The failed candidates never knew that, however. They went on with life.

*Those the elders had their eye on received the same training as did all the other sons of the nobility, who nonetheless were not destined to become candidates for the secret order.*

*The chosen few were taught the secret teachings as fast as they could assimilate them.*

But the chosen few were taught the secret teachings as fast as they could assimilate them.

In many ways, the disciplines of Higher Initiates run parallel to theirs. You, too, learn at your own rate. You also find the right use for your talents and interests.

Being a candidate for Co-workership with God is an enviable position to be in. This is not a game. It is all about love and service.

Yes, the Mahanta, the Living ECK Master loves you. And he'll always meet you more than halfway.

## Chapter Three

# The Mahanta's Love for You

# 8
# The Cage of Life

✦

*E*verything in life has a structure. It changes all the time and has since the dawn of man's arrival on earth as a thinking being.

From his earliest days to the present, man wondered how to protect himself from the forces of nature and the misdeeds of his fellow man that brought him harm. Thus did Soul as the citizen of a harsh, material world seek ways to survive. Time passed, and man's collective experience grew. What did it all mean? Could he mine the helpful knowledge gained and sift from it some precious nuggets to add to what he knew about his origin and the invisible hand of whimsy that often toyed with his happiness and peace of mind?

Man became ever more aware that he was like a creature in a cage. His welfare depended upon a warden, a zookeeper.

This warden was an object of both fear and wonder. He seldom made an appearance. Yet food and water were replenished every day.

Usually.

When either failed to appear, man wondered at the reason. Had he offended the warden? If so,

> *Thus did Soul as the citizen of a harsh, material world seek ways to survive. Time passed, and man's collective experience grew. What did it all mean?*

how? What could man do to appease him and so restore the supply of food and water?

Soul in Its earliest incarnations had but few, if any, of the answers.

Earth was and is a cage. More often referred to as a school, it's a place where all people are to gain experience. With experience comes understanding. It is experience that expands man's mind. The mind, an integral part of man's tools for survival, has great power.

Yet for all that, the mind cannot reach into the spiritual planes.

Man, even the most brilliant of men, is in a cage.

So from earliest history on, man has tried to learn his place in life and how to exist in peace and tranquillity.

As experience began to develop his understanding, man looked about. He asked three questions: What can I know? How should I act? What sort of leader should I choose?

Fear led him to seek knowledge. Since man rubbed shoulders with his neighbors, the next thing he needed to know was some rules of right and wrong. Experience showed that some matters required an outside opinion when he and his neighbor saw right and wrong in a different light. And so a judge arose to fill the need. It may have been one individual or a council of neighbors, but the judge did need to have the force to uphold the court's decision.

As man's development increased, he and his neighbors found moments for reflection. They told

*The mind has great power. Yet for all that, the mind cannot reach into the spiritual planes. Man, even the most brilliant of men, is in a cage.*

stories of those who'd performed acts of uncommon bravery. Those brave deeds were to counteract a threat to a hero's peace and safety.

Such stories became legends and myths.

Through them, man continued on the long road to reach an understanding of his environment and his place in it.

All the while, he was rocked from complacency by events that had no apparent reason to them. So he sought knowledge about earthquakes, freezing snow, lightning, fire, illness, and mostly, about the mystery of death. Birth was natural. It was a common thing to see the entrance of man or beast into the community.

But death was a puzzle. The material form remained, but it no longer acted the way a living being should. And soon it decayed. What set the living apart from the dead?

So man sought knowledge about the things of this world out of fear.

The march of time saw the myths and legends tell of gods. They were like man but invisible, for the most part, yet with more power. Still, even the gods were subject to the Fates. Things they'd set in motion with each other and man sometimes turned out wrong. These gods did not know all things. So they could not enlighten man.

However, that's how man created his gods. They had greater powers than his own, but they too lacked answers to the mysteries that perplexed him.

Man's early gods had few answers for the riddle of life.

*Man's early gods had few answers for the riddle of life.*

Professor Daniel N. Robinson, currently of Oxford University, has an excellent lecture series, *The Great Ideas of Philosophy.* (The Teaching Company, 4151 Lafayette Center Drive, Suite 100, Chantilly, VA 20151-1232; www.teach12.com)

He points to three problems in the history of philosophy: the problem of knowledge, the problem of conduct, and the problem of governance.

Robinson reduces these three problems to everyday questions: What is the world? What should I do? How are our lives to be ordered? Man grapples with these questions. He is ever searching for final answers to them, but they keep slipping through his fingers. They are like wiggling minnows. All man's efforts to catch truth also slip away.

Time and experience add to his longing. For what, he's not sure. But he's certain he'll know it when it appears.

Somewhere along the line he finds the Mahanta, the Living ECK Master. Life has played him the fool so often in his search for truth that man is hesitant about still another teacher. Is it the right one? Is this the anointed of God who can reveal the secret of love and all other mysteries?

Time will tell.

One can only accept as much as his cup of consciousness can hold. Experience is the key. It expands the mind to a greater understanding of the laws that govern his world of matter, space, time, and energy. Yet alone he cannot go beyond that cage of limitations. A Soul that has made spiritual strides via a wealth of experience in the

---

*Alone he cannot go beyond that cage of limitations. A Soul that has made spiritual strides via a wealth of experience in the lower worlds will recognize the Master.*

lower worlds will recognize the Master.

Soon he learns that all the true teachings spring from the Shariyat-Ki-Sugmad, the bible for the ECKist. It exists in the invisible worlds as well as here.

*The Shariyat*, Books One and Two, hold the answers for all the questions that philosophy has raised about the problems of living.

A Higher Initiate wrote to me recently that listening to *The Shariyat* on audio recording adds a whole new dimension to the book. I know you will find it so too.

The Mahanta, the Living ECK Master can free seekers from the downward pull of everyday life. Please help in this mission when the window of opportunity opens. Thank you.

*The Shariyat, Books One and Two, hold the answers for all the questions about the problems of living.*

# 9
# No Charge

There's an old tune in country music that tells a story of unconditional love. It's like the Mahanta's love for you: no charge.

A young boy was required to help out around home as he got older. He had to learn to carry his own weight. Besides making it easier on his parents, it was necessary for him to learn the increasing responsibilities of maturity.

And so the song begins. . . .

One day, the boy handed his mother a sheet of paper. She took it and began to read. On it was a list of duties her son had completed that week, along with the charge for services that he felt were due him.

The duties were of a common sort. For example, making his bed every day that week without being told: $1.00. Raking the lawn: $2.00, etc. At the bottom of the long list of charges, he'd written the total: $14.75. Expectation lit his eyes as he awaited his due reward.

But his mother took the sheet of paper, turned it over, and began to write on this order:

- For all the times I worried and prayed for

*An old tune in country music tells a story of unconditional love. It's like the Mahanta's love for you: no charge.*

you, in sickness, through the night: no charge.
- For all the times I hugged you when you were afraid: no charge.
- For all the times I washed your hurts and put bandages on them: no charge.

And so the mother's list ran until it held many more entries than her son's. She handed the sheet to him. He read of all the times she'd given him love, protection, and understanding. All was done for love. She hadn't wanted or even looked for the slightest reward.

No charge.

Tears clouded his eyes.

"Mama," he said, "I sure do love you."

He then took up the pen, turned the sheet over to his list of charges, and wrote in big letters across his bill: "Paid in full."

Yes, it is a sentimental story. However, it does reflect the Mahanta's love for every Soul, for you. Once you made a commitment to the path of ECK, he was already there by you. He eased your karmic load when you were still too young in spiritual maturity to shoulder it yourself. As you grew in understanding and strength, he let you carry your own weight—more and more, day by day.

*Love has no strings. It allows freedom and responsibility for all.*

Love has no strings. It allows freedom and responsibility for all. Isn't it a fact that SUGMAD (God) has placed each of us in this world so we may become able Co-workers with God? It's the goal of perfection.

That's the reason for our existence, is it not?

Please don't overlook *The Shariyat-Ki-Sugmad*,

Books One and Two, now on audio recordings. Listen to them. They give a new dimension to an understanding of the holy scriptures of ECK.

The Mahanta's love, as you'll hear again in *The Shariyat*, Book One, chapter 6, is even stronger and more lasting than this mother's love for her son. Yes, the Mahanta, the Living ECK Master loves you. He's loved you through all time, through all folly. He expects nothing from you except what you're willing to do in behalf of your own spiritual good.

And he'll always meet you more than halfway.

No charge.

*The Mahanta, the Living ECK Master expects nothing from you except what you're willing to do in behalf of your own spiritual good.*

# 10
# The Master's Enchanting Love

*Divine* love is all-embracing and compelling. The Mahanta, the Living ECK Master's love can enlighten, inspire, and heal. It accounts for the ECK chela's faith and devotion. It is like water drops acting upon rocks.

This holy love breaks down the barriers one has built around him on all sides, keeping it from entering his heart, awakening him.

Such is the nature of true love.

It acts in mysterious ways, confounding the mind and its ability to grasp the changes going on inside. Then love enters. It brings spring to a wintry consciousness, melting it, so that a season of renewal may green the garden to grow the fruits of summer.

Ah, this love is a powerful thing!

And so "Lara" found too.

Lara had unwittingly cut herself off from love for many years. It had left her with no self-confidence, little self-respect, and a tendency to break off friendly relationships, inviting the cold embrace of loneliness. Little wonder that she

*This holy love breaks down the barriers one has built around him on all sides, keeping it from entering his heart, awakening him.*

suffered from depression and sadness.

It all began to change the day Lara met the Living ECK Master while shopping. A veil covered her Spiritual Eye, so she failed to recognize him. She thought, *He looks like a nice man.* Then he was standing by her with his cart. They looked at each other. He commented about some produce, and finally, she recognized him. They embraced.

Stammering, she blurted, "What a blessing!"

From that moment, changes—little ones for now—began to blossom in her life. They were possible because of her new state of consciousness. In due time, more changes will come. Among them, the healing of a troubled heart.

Oh, the enchanting power of love!

\* \* \*

Many of you are ECK Initiators or aspire to be one. Please remember how special the ECK initiations are when *you* are on the receiving end. The same is true for those you initiate in your role as a chosen representative of the Mahanta. This is especially so at ECK major or regional seminars, where you may be called upon to do many initiations. Treat each initiation as a once-in-a-lifetime occasion, for it surely is.

"Ella," a Canadian, received a pink slip for her Third Initiation and soon took it. She is now looking forward to the spiritual lessons and opportunities the Third Circle will present to her.

She recalled the day when after work she had opened the mail and first discovered the Master's invitation into the Third Circle. She was at once honored and humbled.

Later that evening, Ella went out to the porch of her country home to join her daughter's boyfriend. The night was dark and still. And yet, the air was charged with the ECK all around them. He sensed something, so she told him of having received very good news that day and left it at that.

Curiosity overcame him.

"May I ask what it was?" he said.

She told him about the ECK initiation. He was aware that she is an ECKist and was not opposed to it.

"In ECKANKAR," she said, "it is earning the privilege to move on to the next spiritual step and gain the capacity for more love."

The two stood there quietly pondering and looking out into the beautiful evening full of stars.

The air was ever so still.

Then the wind chimes beside them began to sway gently and ring in the charged air, about six times. Ella knew it for the Sound of ECK. Looking over at him, she saw that this was also a special moment for him, although he remained unsure of how the chimes had begun to ring without a wind, or what it all meant.

Ella explained, "God and the Holy Spirit are always communicating with us, and sometimes we are too busy to notice. But when we are quiet and receptive, we become aware of it, like in this case of the chimes ringing."

She further explained that God (SUGMAD) is always here for us—even if we do not see Him—and that He loves us.

"That ringing," she said, "signifies that some-

*The wind chimes beside them began to sway gently and ring in the charged air, about six times. Ella knew it for the Sound of ECK.*

thing has 'rung true' for us."

He stood quietly thinking over what she had said and was visibly moved by this experience. Ella knew it for the Mahanta's blessing upon both of them.

It was one enchanted evening.

With the Light and Sound shining and singing inside your heart, all around you will see nobility in duty as a spiritual advantage.

Chapter Four

# How to Be a Better Vehicle for ECK

# 11

# A Change in Consciousness—Not an Overnight Event

An astute observer once said, "A man convinced against his will is of the same opinion still."

Oh, how true! No matter what we think, we're of the same mind. When someone presses his ideas on us, we are likely to feel some resistance, because most of us don't like somebody telling us what to do. We may smile agreeably and nod our heads. But once the other is gone, we do as we please. Out of sight, out of mind.

There is an exception, though. It's when there's a clear benefit in our favor. Then we're quick to grab the chance. And why not? Like most anybody else, we move toward whatever affords us a more pleasant life.

So do you see what we're getting at?

It is change, of course. We prefer the known to the unknown. Forget about change! All too often, in our experience, it has brought nothing but trouble in one way or another. And funny thing,

*An astute observer once said, "A man convinced against his will is of the same opinion still."*

isn't it, how unpleasant experiences seem to stick in our minds better than pleasant ones? It is just a part of our nature.

Sheri, who had worked in a large supermarket for fifteen years, learned an uncomfortable lesson about choosing stability over a chance to move on and learn new skills.

"I knew I'd stayed there too long," Sheri confessed, "when I dreaded leaving my car and going inside." So she quit.

Her new job was at a health-food co-op. Sheri didn't know the first thing about organic goods, but a job was a job. Both management and customers taught her the benefits of organic foods; some people had overcome annoying or even severe health problems.

She was recently offered the opportunity to move to a new store location.

"I've been here six years," she said. "I'm not making the same mistake again." Sheri has the adventurous spirit of many ECKists, although she isn't one yet.

So we welcome change when it offers us a clear advantage over our present situation.

The same is true for many who come to ECKANKAR from another religion or path. They've tried the rest. Then they come to ECK, which speaks to them now. Something in the ECK teachings rings true in their hearts.

A missionary once observed, "You don't change a man's religion in twenty minutes."

He recognized that people don't make a sudden, apparently total change in their belief system

*We welcome change when it offers us a clear advantage over our present situation.*

# A Change in Consciousness—Not an Overnight Event

unless the experiences of life have already nudged them far enough along in that direction. Even then, the suddenness of their decision often shocks those near to them.

An ECKist told me that when she first encountered ECKANKAR, she knew it was what she'd been born for. Soul knew and was ready to go home to God.

Change for her, in this case, was a highly desirable spiritual step. She's never looked back.

The ECK Master tells the seeker in *Stranger by the River* of an age-old law of God. "The law of God," he says, "compels man to see Him, and you must know that even though you may never seek God, He will seek you and compel you to turn to Him."

It was a gradual change in consciousness in the seeker that accounted for his meeting with the ECK Master.

Such is the nature of spiritual unfoldment.

To repeat, "A man convinced against his will is of the same opinion still."

A long time ago in ECKANKAR, a number of members were too much the evangelist. They lacked the spiritual discrimination to tell who was ready for ECK and who was not. They pushed themselves upon people. They played on people's goodwill not to be rude in rebuffing them. I hope this wild spirit of evangelism is on the wane. There are signs it is.

A doctor of alternative healing in the Minneapolis area is a strong Christian, but many of his patients are ECKists. He's impressed by them.

*It was a gradual change in consciousness in the seeker that accounted for his meeting with the ECK Master.*

"They don't try to convert me," he says.

Many ECKists know that a change in consciousness is not usually an overnight event. When it is appropriate, they tell others of the ECK teachings. Otherwise, they keep still and go about their business.

They're living the high principle of ECK, to let others enjoy their spiritual beliefs. So remember, "A man convinced against his will is of the same opinion still."

*A change in consciousness is not usually an overnight event.*

# 12
# War, Peace, and the Task of ECKANKAR

*W*ay back when, Joan once asked how to be a more effective instrument for ECK.

For an overview, I said it was important to understand the most compelling needs of Soul, and the answer for that was in *The Shariyat-Ki-Sugmad*. A spiritual overview of a problem about humankind is a necessary starting point. *The Shariyat* is always the place to go first.

It says: "Many of the arguments which develop into war between men have arisen out of arguments over the definitions and incarnations of God" (Book Two).

By the latest count, man is waging war against a neighbor in some fifty or more conflicts worldwide. So where does this leave a peacenik, a pacifist? Is he engaged in a lose-lose endeavor? Ask him. Fooled by the great illusionist Kal Niranjan, the pacifist acts to create situations that sprout even more discord among people. An example is the belief that the disarmament of a force with superior strength will bring peace to all concerned.

*To be a more effective instrument for ECK, a spiritual overview of a problem about humankind is a necessary starting point.*

There's a problem with this theory. The fact is that history shows its failure to succeed.

What's the reason for its failure?

As long as envy, deceit, and contention remain in even a single human breast, there will never be peace among men. Of course, some will argue the point. However, isn't that a proof in itself about the contentious nature of mankind? It loves argument and discord.

No decree by man or beast will change that.

Joan's expression after my explanation seemed to beg for an insight into something more relevant to the immediate teaching and practice of the ECK principles. But there was a further thought to consider.

World War I at its end, I said, was the largest war ever recorded in history. The winners, aware of the terrible cost in human life, wanted only to put the whole unpleasant episode from their lives. So with full confidence in the human mind to create a condition that would forever stop the outbreak of further such destruction, they looked for the end of future global warfare.

"The war to end all wars" became almost a prayer in the hearts of people tired of senseless carnage.

The sad irony is that many who suffered from World War I saw more big wars—World War II, the Korean War, the war in Vietnam, and the continuation of many smaller firefights around the globe.

So what went wrong with the dream?

Nobody fixed the human consciousness. No

*As long as envy, deceit, and contention remain in even a single human breast, there will never be peace among men.*

single war or collection of wars has addressed the underlying problem: man's refusal to live according to the high principles of ECK. He will not permit the Light and Sound of God to enter his heart and guide his behavior toward his fellows.

And do you know what?

He cannot. The whole secret is that no single war or collection of them can ever bring a lasting change to the human consciousness.

And do you know something else?

Neither can the human will, either singly or as a mandate from any group of human masterminds who propose a solution according to their own lights. Their bulbs are too dim. So the game of illusion runs on and on.

Now this could leave us facing a pretty grim prospect.

What does it mean? Is it senseless to strive for peace, for goodwill among men?

No, in fact it's man's saving grace. Human efforts to achieve peace and harmony show that a spark of divine consciousness does yet burn beneath the ashes of man's spiritual campfire, which, on the face of it, looks cold and dead.

What I'm saying, though, is that such efforts be directed in the right place. That place is one's *own* heart.

Have you noticed when the "disciples of peace" go on a mission it's to make other people change *their* states of consciousness? A pacifist believes he's already arrived at the ultimate state. So, what's to change at home?

The answer, to the audiences of Kal, the great

*The underlying problem: man's refusal to permit the Light and Sound of God to enter his heart and guide his behavior toward his fellows.*

illusionist, is: nothing. And that's the mistake. Reform must start at home, in one's own heart. This means, too, the right sort of change.

A change to a higher state of consciousness must occur in each heart. No exceptions.

Further, a change to a higher state alone is not enough. Unless it arrives at the *highest* state, the wars among mankind will not, cannot, abate.

So, where do you go and what do you do?

Back to *The Shariyat*!

In Book Two it speaks of the ECK as the living power that exists behind creation. It governs all creativity. Yet when man rejects the Spirit of God, he, at the same time, becomes one who practices the destructive powers of the Kal Niranjan, the negative force. It stands in opposition to the divine will.

In short, one is either a disciple of the ECK or of the Kal.

So it is necessary to strive for harmony. But one must take the right road. Change begins at home.

The Kal consciousness, you see, is the reason for man's weakness and misery. It's a destructive force. *The Shariyat* adds: "This brings the war that splits him, raging within him, and makes him the battlefield between the ECK and Kal forces within the consciousness of the individual."

And note, this warfare is due to man's refusal to live according to the will of the divine power, the ECK.

Here, then, is *the most important task of ECKANKAR*. It is "to bend and restring the bow of Soul by proper training and discipline."

---

*A change to a higher state of consciousness must occur in each heart. No exceptions.*

May I urge you to read *The Shariyat*, Book Two, chapter 5? You'll refresh your memory about the sacred word of HU, because it is the key to restoring the confidence of Soul. First, HU sweeps out the cobwebs of useless and misleading theology. It rids the consciousness of errant ideas about the purpose of life on earth, never intended to be a garden of paradise except in the sense of a spiritual classroom without equal.

Second, HU can once more "be attached to the Spiritual Exercises of ECK" once the teachings of ECK have a firm footing in the individual.

On the surface, then, one sees only the single action of chanting HU. Yet two separate actions occur.

This explains the emphasis in ECK on singing the HU song. Only HU can clear the heart of dross and rejuvenate the spiritual consciousness in a compelling and lasting way.

No, this poor, tired old earth will never see peace among men. But an ECKist can find peace and love even in the cold, dark cellars of hell.

Joan knows this, and so do most of you.

*Only HU can clear the heart of dross and rejuvenate the spiritual consciousness in a compelling and lasting way.*

# 13
# Bring In the Candles

※

A chela from St. Louis, Missouri (the "Show Me" State), sent a story from an old school reader. The story was in a letter from General Robert E. Lee, the brilliant leader of the Confederate army during the American Civil War of the 1860s.

The letter was to his son, G. W. Custis Lee, who was at college. The introduction in the school reader noted the significance of General Lee's counsel:

"The letter contains such good advice from an eminent father to his son that we are naturally anxious to read it closely. The incident told of the old Puritan legislator is one of the best illustrations we have of faithful adherence to duty."

General Lee advised his son to be frank with the world. And, as the ECK chela pointed out, he gave the very same advice contained in Maybury's two laws. Again, for your review, the seventeen words of the latter are these:

"Do all you have agreed to do, and do not encroach on other persons or their property."

General Lee said it like this: "Frankness is the child of honesty and courage. Say just what you mean to do, on every occasion, and take it for granted

*General Lee advised his son to be frank with the world.*

you mean to do right. If a friend asks a favor, you should grant it, if it is reasonable; if not, tell him plainly why you cannot; you would wrong him and wrong yourself by equivocation of any kind."

The old general's sound advice came from a true and noble heart. Even his enemies during the war bestowed their respect upon him, for he was a man set apart.

Lee added: "Never do a wrong thing to make a friend or keep one; the man who requires you to do so is dearly purchased at the sacrifice. . . . Above all, do not appear to others what you are not."

All good advice, especially in these times of equivocation, of political correctness, etc. Today's sorry situation comes because small hearts and minds have driven honor and nobility from the scene. People no longer have the courage to be honest with themselves, because there's so little in them to be proud of.

People have lost their way. They've lost it spiritually, and all their other endeavors reflect that lost and wandering state.

General Lee advised his son to "live, act, and say nothing to the injury of any one."

Then, in regard to duty, he told the story of the old Puritan lawmaker, and it applies equally in ECKANKAR as well as in world society.

In the mid 1700s, said Lee, a day of remarkable gloom and darkness befell the land. It was still known during General Lee's day, nearly one hundred years later, as "the dark day." The light of the sun slowly diminished until day was as night.

The legislature of Connecticut was in session

*He told the story of the old Puritan lawmaker, and it applies equally in ECKANKAR as well as in world society.*

at the time. Its members felt terror at the unaccountable darkness, and some supposed the judgment day had arrived.

With that awful prospect in mind, one of the legislators made a motion to adjourn.

But an old Puritan legislator arose and addressed the assembly. If the last day had truly come, he said, he wished to be found at his place of duty. Instead of adjourning, he made a motion to bring in the candles so that the house could continue with its duty.

Lee observed a quietness in that legislator's mind, born of "the quietness of heavenly wisdom and inflexible willingness to obey present duty."

So bring in the candles.

The light they shed are of the Light and Sound. Their rays carry to the dark corners of the world, lighting and enlivening all by their presence. And, thus, the right attention to duty may be fulfilled. With the Light and Sound shining and singing inside your heart, all around you will see nobility in duty as a spiritual advantage.

Duty. Doing the right thing. Guidelines with which to do one's duty in ECK spiritually, in the right way, for the benefit of all.

And yet some H.I.'s are heard to carp about duty as given by the spiritual hierarchy. These H.I.'s have lost their way in the darkness of their inner lands. Bring in the candles. Let the Light and Sound of God shed light upon their darkened paths of wandering.

One who knows the delicate and beautiful workings of the human body understands that its

*Duty. Doing the right thing. Guidelines with which to do one's duty in ECK spiritually, in the right way, for the benefit of all.*

systems and organs must work in accord with its hierarchy.

Can the heart set its beat without regard to the strength of the blood vessels? Can the kidneys ignore the capacity of the bladder? Or the mind ignore the physical condition of the muscles and decree too much exercise for an overburdened heart?

No, the members and systems of your body do their best to work in harmony with each other.

A nerve impulse that continually spurts hydrochloric acid into the stomach before the arrival of food will burn out the stomach lining. Is it so hard to see?

All life exists in an intricate and delicate structure, for such is the Creator's design. What petty human will has grown itself into such importance to lay aside the scheme of creation and put itself at the center of it all? Can vanity go to such lengths among even some higher initiates in ECKANKAR?

Of concern, too, are some ECK leaders—including a few RESAs, who willfully ignore the guidelines for the ECK Worship Services. They let Second and Third initiates conduct the services even when the area has sufficient ECK clergy or Fourth and Fifth initiates in training to be ECK clergy.

The two above-named problems are the same blight at heart. These initiates have contrived to push the Mahanta, the Living ECK Master from the picture. In his place, they set themselves.

Is it any wonder there is a spiritual darkness in the land?

*Can vanity go to such lengths among even some higher initiates in ECKANKAR?*

General Lee had a final bit of advice for his son. "If you have any fault to find with any one, tell him, not others, of what you complain; there is no more dangerous experiment than that of undertaking to be one thing before a man's face and another behind his back."

And thus spoke a very wise man. So let's bring in the candles.

*So let's bring in the candles.*

A discerning eye will see the winds of ECK (Holy Spirit) filling and emptying the sails of our ships so we land in the right place, at the right time.

## Chapter Five

# Tests and Challenges of the Higher Initiate

# 14
# Nothing Succeeds like Failure

"Failure" is a funny word. All of us have faced it in one way or another, either now or then. But it's a natural part of living.

What follows a setback, however, is not equal. Sometimes we get up to try again; other times, after a string of failures hit us, we surrender and give up all. That is a true failure.

Unless—

Unless, of course, we slide out from beneath that series of crushing blows and put our might into a fresh endeavor.

We thus set out on a new venture.

If the result of that change is to our liking, gives us a sense of purpose and happiness, then the whole bundle of past failures is wiped from the slate. Success has a way of blunting prior failures.

The *Wall Street Journal* (Jan. 16, 2001) ran an article on a recent change in approach among motivational speakers ("For Motivational Speakers, Nothing Succeeds Like Failure").

*"Failure" is a funny word. All of us have faced it in one way or another, either now or then.*

The old approach was rah-rah. It worked, giving professional speechmakers a good source of income.

Then, disaster. The stock market crashed.

Within a few short months attendance at motivational seminars dropped off. The speakers were missing their audience.

They found the reason. A lot of people had lost a lot of money in the stock market. Stacks of money meant for retirement had gone poof. And as investors faced loss instead of largesse from the markets, their interest in tales of wild success waned.

Bottom line: audiences shrank.

Bottom-bottom line: Speechmakers were in a money squeeze too.

Oh, what to do? What to do?

Something new, dear friends. Something new.

And so a marked change took place. Motivational speakers who first saw the problem went to fix it. If people were losing money and felt like failures, the speakers had to go down to their level and pick them up.

Motivational speeches saw innovation. Speakers now began with a story about defeat. That perked up ears. When they had the attention and interest of the group, they told how someone reeling from a setback had picked himself up and taken a new direction. To success. Failure was not a life sentence. It was but a stop along the way to success and happiness.

And thus the top speechmakers averted their own ruin.

*Oh, what to do? What to do? Something new, dear friends. Something new.*

A sidebar to this article gave a few examples of the old approach to motivational speaking versus the new.

**Old:** "How I made it big." **New:** "How I learned from big mistakes."

**Old:** "Litany of bright moments." **New:** "My darkest hour."

**Old:** "Unswerving success." **New:** "Rebounds."

\* \* \*

When troubles befall them, people need spiritual help. ECK presentations, too, reach others better when stories or examples of failure and how you picked yourself up and moved on are sprinkled throughout a talk. Life is not a string of rah-rah moments. It gives both hugs and bruises.

Life serves up bitters and sweets. The sweets keep us in the game. The challenge is to "Know thyself." What wall once stopped you from realizing a goal? What bitter reality knocked you to your knees?

What's more, what sweet moment of truth caused you to struggle back up? A smile? A word of kindness? Or someone's ready ear?

(An American Indian proverb has it thus: Listen or thy tongue will keep thee deaf.)

This letter to you is the result of listening to moans of despair from those who've faced big losses. And these losses can be from something other than the slide in the stock market. Life gives and life takes. That's the nature of it—even as it was the nature of all our past lives.

Investors may hold false hopes about the stock

*Life serves up bitters and sweets. The sweets keep us in the game. The challenge is to "Know thyself."*

market. They *hope* it will restore their paper riches. Chances are, it'll tease them with rebounds and bigger slides until all their retirement moneys vanish.

The markets offer a false hope, a false security.

Where then is real security?

In spiritual things. In treasures not of this world.

*Where then is real security? In spiritual things. In treasures not of this world.*

\* \* \*

A certain health practitioner gave a talk on healing at a chamber of commerce. It fell flat. Of some fifty or more members in attendance, only one person asked for more information about the health services provided.

One, just one member.

This doctor has an excellent record of up to a 50 percent response from other audiences.

In analyzing the poor result with the chamber of commerce, the doctor noted how little interest they paid to the threat of, say, electromagnetic radiation in the workplace.

This was a group of scrambling businesspeople. Their concerns were sales, taxes, litigation, and competition. Real threats. Not vague ones like subtle electrical waves from computers, fans, or fluorescent lights.

Their problems gave the business leaders a big headache.

Headache?

A light went on in the doctor's head. So tell them about treatments to reduce stress and headaches!

The doctor may try to speak to that group again.

\* \* \*

In ECK, we offer spiritual aid to those who've taken a beating from life. HU, the love song to God, is a divine hug, a sweet. Give that to those on their knees. It can help them up on their feet.

Success in all areas of life comes with the Spiritual Exercises of ECK. Do them.

It's as Ralph Waldo Emerson, the poet, said, "Skill to do comes of doing."

*HU, the love song to God, is a divine hug, a sweet. Give that to those on their knees. It can help them up on their feet.*

# 15
# Look for the Gifts!

A vacation can be a wonderful opportunity to see how the Mahanta will make things work out. Of course, you must do your part too.

Everything is fresh during a vacation, though often fraught with challenges, obstacles, and irritants. But it all depends upon your outlook. A spiritual exercise is to look for the gifts cloaked inside your experiences, because the gifts exist as potential realities.

So look for the gifts!

To demonstrate this, let us look in on the summer vacation of "Nan" and her husband, "Bert." They took a trip to the Czech Republic. Bert's parents live there, and they treated the travelers like royalty. Since Bert's parents live in the country, it gave Nan a chance to seek peace and quiet, of which her job offers so little. Each morning, Nan got to walk in the woods. There, she would do her contemplation.

Nan would seat herself on her special "contemplation log" in the woods. First, she would read from *Those Wonderful ECK Masters*, then do her ECK Spiritual Exercises, and finally, work on her seminar talks. What an idyllic setting!

*A spiritual exercise is to look for the gifts cloaked inside your experiences, because the gifts exist as potential realities. So look for the gifts!*

Yet life will often sing us another tune, like the old country song "(I Never Promised You a) Rose Garden." It is like finding a dill pickle in your ice cream, a worm in your apple, or a bug in your milk. In short, a cloud before your sun.

A theme of one of her talks was recognizing the love of God in all things in your life. The vacation gave many opportunities for Nan to practice what she preached.

On the second day after their arrival, Nan and Bert went into town for groceries. When they emerged from the store, a man came up to them.

He said, "Someone hit your car and drove off!"

Indeed, their rental car had a dent and paint scraped off the bumper. A small part of the side of the car saw light damage too. Their credit card, they thought, would cover it. However, they were not sure about possible deductibles.

The witness, from France, had written down the license number, which proved to be from another country.

Bert and Nan immediately took this information to the police station. But the language barrier was an insurmountable wall. The couple and police kept making gestures and were shrugging at each other. In the meantime, the hit-and-run driver was able to make a clean getaway.

Things looked bleak. However, in contemplation, Nan remembered what she had read in *Those Wonderful ECK Masters*. It was to let things be; to do our best, then surrender the matter to the Mahanta.

So she and Bert determined not to let the

---

*Nan remembered what she had read in* Those Wonderful ECK Masters. *It was to let things be; to do our best, then surrender the matter to the Mahanta.*

incident spoil their vacation.

Bert's father later accompanied them to the police station to act as interpreter. The police were very thorough. They filled out a complete police report, took photos, noted details surrounding the accident, and the like. But they said there was no hope of finding the man who had hit them.

But the gift was this: the credit-card people were very nice. They said their company would cover everything as part of their service.

Nan later saw that the theme for their vacation was to work together to solve situations. It was no use getting upset or pointing fingers. That only interfered with the help the ECK was trying to provide. That was an all-important lesson.

Nan's next misadventure also involved shopping for food. The store was big and overcrowded. Nan paid for her few purchases. Then she noticed that her wallet was missing. She and Bert looked high and low for it, but it was nowhere to be found. The blessing lay in the fact that the wallet was old. She had planned to toss it out after their vacation. Anyway, the only things in it were a list of phone numbers and a bandage. She always carried her cash in separate pouches.

Nan concluded, "If it *had* been stolen, maybe the person really needed a Band-Aid."

The flight from Prague home to the United States was aborted due to mechanical difficulties. By the time the couple reached Amsterdam, they had missed their flight to Minneapolis. It looked like one more setback. But wait!

The gift they received was entirely welcome.

*It looked like one more setback. But wait! The gift they received was entirely welcome.*

The airline put them up overnight in a four-star hotel, provided a shuttle bus, an overnight care package, international phone calls, a three-course dinner, a buffet, and vouchers for future trips. Nan and Bert also caught a train into Amsterdam for a couple hours of sightseeing. It was an extra vacation day. Plus, due to the time change, Nan made it to work the day of the flight home.

So take a vacation! Throw yourself upon the mercies of life. Stay open to the ECK. Avoid the blame game of pointing fingers and making judgments. And have fun.

*So take a vacation! Throw yourself upon the mercies of life. Stay open to the ECK. And have fun.*

# 16
# A Pot of Gold or Something Greater?

There is a fox outside the henhouse, and it bears watching. You are a guardian of the henhouse, helping your RESA in making sure the ECK chelas in your area receive fair treatment from those who are above them in some service to ECK.

These lovers of truth and the Mahanta, the Living ECK Master deserve fair treatment. Most ECK leaders show them that courtesy.

However, a few do not.

Much of the ECK work is borne by chelas who do so out of pure love. There is no remuneration involved. Their spiritual blessings are great, far greater even than receiving a pot of gold filled to the brim. So they represent love.

The fox stands for power. He is ruthless and sees a house full of chicken dinners. He feeds on the weak and helpless, on those who cannot defend themselves.

Now, what kind of a guardian would it be who stood by and let the fox, a power seeker, satisfy his pleasure?

Someone who knows what is going on, is in

*There is a fox outside the henhouse, and it bears watching. The fox stands for power.*

a position to do something about it, but purposely shuts his eyes to the problem—out of fear, perhaps, of offending the perpetrator—is an accomplice of the fox.

How could he not be?

I was thinking about this constant struggle that exists between love and power, even among ECKists. You look at such people with their goose-stepping tactics and you wonder about them. Sometimes they almost seem to be schizophrenic, with opposing or antagonistic sides.

On one hand, they are ever so loving and helpful. But on the other, they are tromping on the rights of others with big, muddy boots. Yet they can't see themselves.

Don't we all find it easier to spot a blemish in another instead of ourselves?

Behind the big boots is the ego. It is out of control and can thus do a great deal of harm. These goose-stepping people love power, not love. It is disheartening to see them. They intrude into the domain of others. Deep within a file cabinet they come across a vague rule that, if taken out of context, says the others are not in compliance with it.

This steps on people lower in the pecking order, who must keep silent.

Long ago, as a Vahana in the field, I happened into a neighboring Mahdis's area to give an introductory lecture. This was in the old days, when the rules were not always drafted very well.

That Mahdis complained to the ECK Office. So I found that the better part of valor was discretion, and thus wisely kept out of that area.

What struck me was that the area wasn't growing!

This Mahdis used up so much energy protecting her turf that she had neither the time nor energy to do an adequate job of ECK Vahana work in her very populous area. It was sad. She would not do it and acted like a bucket of cold water when others did show initiative.

One such person can do so much damage to an organization, especially to one like ECKANKAR, because it places a lot of faith in volunteers and their love for the Master.

These foxes—power eaters—are extremely stubborn in their determination to dominate others. If they could only see themselves.

Their motto: "My way or the highway."

Other approaches they favor include becoming overly familiar with an intended victim. Then they take control of the other's life. The goose-stepper, the fox, is thus guilty of violating the ECK precept of allowing others to have their freedom.

Such a person thinks his ego is under control as much as that of another. He licks the boots of those above him in the hierarchy and expects those below him to lick his. He is truly schizophrenic. He and his like are few in number, but they do so much damage to the ECK missionary effort. They are like an atomic bomb exploding over a city.

You may get reports of a fox operating in a Satsang class, as someone in charge of ECK intro talks, or in other important ECK activities. Keep your eyes and ears open. Find out if anything is

*An organization like ECKANKAR places a lot of faith in volunteers and their love for the Master.*

behind the rumors, and inform the local ECK leadership or the RESA.

Keep in mind that ECK chelas are precious Souls. They deserve love and respect. They're serving ECK out of love, not for a pot of gold. Sweep the way clear of a fox. Allow the ECK chelas to serve. Let them unfold, so that their spiritual reward can be greater than any pot of gold.

*Keep in mind that ECK chelas are precious Souls. They deserve love and respect.*

# 17

# In God's Time

A Higher Initiate asked for an insight into a series of reverses he'd been seeing in his personal and business affairs.

"Jim," let's say, rightly felt the finger of responsibility pointed back at him. But what was he overlooking? Was there a spiritual principle that would set him on track again? If so, what and where was it?

On the business side of the ledger, incredible things had happened in his last few positions that looked for all the world a bit demonic. A subordinate, in one case, undermined Jim's credibility with the company's head. He smiled to Jim's face but cut him to ribbons behind his back, which led to Jim's dismissal from the company. To add salt to Jim's wounds, this liar was promoted to replace him. There were other, similar setbacks too.

On the home front, he was trying to sell a piece of real estate, but deal after deal fell through. The repeated delays cost him much peace of mind. Because, as time marched on, his savings were running out. Eventually, when his back was against the wall, the real estate sale closed, and that nightmare was over.

*A Higher Initiate asked for insight into a series of reverses. Was there a spiritual principle that would set him on track again?*

Jim's personal relationships were troublesome too. Promising ones collapsed, leaving him in the dust.

All in all, he decided there must be a better way.

Joan, at the time, was researching "beingness" in the ECK writings. So when Jim's request for spiritual insight on his problems came to me, it was at a perfect time. The ECK had set Joan to work on the research right before Jim's letter arrived.

This principle of synchronicity applies to timing and events, and a discerning eye will see the winds of ECK (Holy Spirit) filling and emptying the sails of our ships so we land in the right place, at the right time.

The name for this spiritual phenomenon is "In God's Time."

In God's time. In God's time.

When it gets right down to it, all events in life occur in God's time. There is no mistake, no accident. Good and evil play their part in the divine scheme of giving everyone the right thing at the right time. We, and all our plans, fit into place on the divine calendar.

Most people pass through this life in an unconscious spiritual state. They are life's victims. They spend so much time and effort trying to lay the blame for their unhappy lives upon others.

Jim, however, is in the awakened state. He knows what he knows, and what he does not know. And he is lifetimes ahead of many—most—people around him. Moreover, he knows where to

*The name for this spiritual phenomenon is "In God's Time." We, and all our plans, fit into place on the divine calendar.*

look for answers to the many things still beyond his reach. He instinctively turns to the Mahanta, the Living ECK Master.

And so his request for assistance came in my mail.

*The Flute of God* by Paul Twitchell contains the answers he was seeking. The information is in four chapters, which follow:

In chapter 6, "The Unknown Name of God," look for references to "the method of creation." There will also be other references in "the radiating HU," and "the key."

In chapter 8, "The Appeal of Man to God," look for the principles of acceptance and manifestation.

In chapter 9, "The Shape of the Altar," there's guidance on how to work harmoniously with the Law of Consciousness. It speaks of why some find life hard, because they refuse gifts offered with love. Yet those who respond to the law find it easy to make contact with God.

In chapter 12, "The Borders of Heaven," there is revealed the reason for keeping your focus on the good and desirable, the harmonious and beautiful, to bring it into form. And why it's vital to avoid negative thoughts and words.

These sections show how to move beyond victimhood and turn all your endeavors toward self-mastery.

Herein lie the keys to the insights Jim had asked of the Master. I know some of you will profit from the same information too.

By now, many of you have located a copy of

> *The Flute of God by Paul Twitchell contains the answers he was seeking. These sections show how to move beyond victimhood and turn all your endeavors toward self-mastery.*

Dale Carnegie's *How to Win Friends and Influence People*. It's well worth reading.

An H.I. once said she'd expected more information on how to reach the higher states of consciousness, but she didn't want to hear more about daily life and the spiritual lessons it teaches us.

In a profound way, it's inconceivable that a high-level initiate of so many years still would not have made the connection between life on earth as the divine route to higher states of consciousness.

It's practically beyond belief that one with such ideas would remain in ECKANKAR.

Life here is a rare and precious opportunity.

Most Higher Initiates have seen the proof of it again and again over the years. In fact, the ECK teachings and its tenets of karma and reincarnation give a plausible insight into the joys and reverses on earth. We can go well beyond the orthodox religionist's belief that when disaster strikes, it is the will of God.

Of course, it is. But we can know *why* it strikes. The ECK teachings reveal our role in the events that buoy our spirits or dash them into the ground. In ECK, our past lives are playing cards turned faceup on the table.

Always appreciate the unique insights you've gained from the teachings of ECK. Revere them, for they are holy things.

And to the few who still don't understand the mission or teachings of the Mahanta, the Living ECK Master, I say, "Persevere. In God's time you will see and know all."

*The ECK teachings reveal our role in the events that buoy our spirits or dash them into the ground.*

The majority of you do understand them and realize that this life's experiences are a great blessing. To you, I heartily recommend *How to Win Friends and Influence People*. A person of self-responsibility senses that his daily behavior causes a lot of problems for him. Most of them are unnecessary. This book shows *how* to treat others with the respect and dignity that befits all God's children.

I urge you to read only a few pages of the book at a time. Take the opportunity to practice along the way what you're learning.

And note that all does come to us in God's time.

> How to Win Friends and Influence People *shows how to treat others with the respect and dignity that befits all God's children.*

A passage from the Shariyat can serve like a lighthouse. Its beam will cut the dark. Then warm yet piercing light spreads balm upon an aching heart.

# Chapter Six

# Overcoming Illusion

# 18
# Home Is Where the Heart Is

My childhood was blessed with two wonderful people. Aunts Clara and Lena were second parents to us kids. They were Mother's sisters. All three had grown up on a farm within half a mile of home that was visible across the fields until our corn grew too tall.

They had come to our place each weekend since before we were born. And every so often, they made an unexpected midweek visit to help Mother feed ten or twenty workers, make sausage at butchering time, or help in the garden. It delighted us.

Both remained single, but their visits continued as regularly as the four seasons. They soon built a new home in town some twenty miles away, nearer their work. It was a considerable distance to drive on country roads, especially so in winter. Their new home, however, proved a blessing due to a special occasion or two besides their weekly farm visits.

The big event was dinner at their home on New Year's Day. Friends and relatives gathered for the lavish banquet of turkey, cranberries (a personal favorite of mine), several kinds of pie,

*My childhood was blessed with two wonderful people. Aunts Clara and Lena were second parents to us kids.*

cakes, and all the soda pop we could wash down.

Afternoons saw the men playing sheepshead, a card game. The women watched the Rose Parade before the Rose Bowl football game. We kids sat around a big table in the basement also playing sheepshead with our cousins and other friends.

New Year's was truly a magical day.

Time marched on. Aunts Clara and Lena came to our farm as often as of old. Even when I left the farm near age thirty, the warmth of their visits remained unchanging from my birth onward. They were like second parents in every possible way.

Without knowing it, I'd come to associate them with our place and theirs. They animated both our farm and their snug and inviting home with their presence.

Some years later, both aunts died. I'd long since moved to other parts of the country and hadn't had the pleasure of seeing them. And then they were gone! With them the golden aura that had so enlivened our homes went out. My brother put their house up for sale. There was no longer a point to keeping their empty, fifty-year-old place.

Then I finally realized a great truth: a house is not a home. A house is but a house. It's simply a place. What a revelation for me!

That's all, just a place.

It's every bit as empty as a human body at death. Just a vacant thing.

A certain location occupied by the same family gives a sense of permanence as one generation blends into the following one. The coming of babies and the going of elders feeds a sense of solidarity.

*With them the golden aura that had so enlivened our homes went out. Then I finally realized a great truth: a house is not a home. A house is but a house. It's simply a place.*

Yes, and certainly one of permanence. So it's a comforting thing, but it's only an illusion. Nothing more.

It's the reason for some oft-repeated sayings, which you may know as well as your own name. One says, "There's no place like home." Oh, how true!

The same holds true for "Home sweet home." It bestows an air of goodness and consideration amid kind and patient hearts. And may it ever be so.

Let's also keep in mind "Home is where the heart is."

Unfortunately, the average person equates "home" with speaking of his body. He's come to believe that Soul and his body are one and the same thing, but he's widely off the mark. He's shooting arrows into the wild.

And what comes of such a misguided belief? He's afraid to die. His whole life, as a result, is run by fear, a fear of dying.

All ECKists should have passed that stage. Our life is certainly precious. It is a marvelous chance to learn and grow, so we do everything possible to stay in our bodies. And it is a wonderful opportunity here to gain spiritually.

This lifetime in ECK is a priceless gift. It is also the key to a true understanding of "Home is where the heart is."

*This lifetime in ECK is a priceless gift. It is also the key to a true understanding of "Home is where the heart is."*

# 19

# The Gift of the Eternal Teachings

*A* good day to you!

As I sit here thinking about you, it comes to mind how so many in ECK know and appreciate the gift of the eternal teachings. *The Shariyat-Ki-Sugmad*, Books One and Two, are a treasure trove. When troubles come hard and fast, they offer a penetrating look at the spiritual fabric of living.

Clearly, they cut through the confusion of the hour.

Fear and passion do have the awesome power to let one feel cut off from the love of SUGMAD, or God. But a passage from the Shariyat can serve like a lighthouse. Its beam will cut the dark.

Then warm yet piercing light spreads balm upon an aching heart.

Once, a host of worries had enwrapped me like a dip in taffy. It happened that on my way to the post office along a winding, tree- and bush-lined road, a rabbit appeared ahead, off to the side. It looked uncertain about its course of action. Seconds later, another car approached from the other direction.

*A passage from the Shariyat can serve like a lighthouse. Its beam will cut the dark.*

I immediately took my foot from the accelerator and poised it over the brake. Animals have a habit of testing a driver's reaction time.

True to form, without so much as a nod to tip his intentions, Brother Rabbit darted onto the roadway directly in front of my car, the closer of the two. I tapped the brakes, and he narrowly escaped with a tall tale (nearly shortened) to awe his prodigious offspring.

Such was his tale, but what lesson was in it for me?

Whenever an out-of-the-ordinary event comes along to jolt our awareness, it pays to look again, and more closely. This was a waking dream, of course. Yet what could its meaning be?

Some American Indian tribes regarded a rabbit appearing in a dream or vision as a symbol of fear. Yes, my worries were a mask for fear.

So how did the scene of this rabbit darting into the road play out? What was the interpretation of the waking dream created for my benefit by the ECK, Divine Spirit? It was all quite simple to decipher once I realized that the incident was a waking dream: sharp like a dream, but I was awake.

Here was its meaning: Let fear go.

Quick and simple. Just let it go.

An image then came to mind of myself many years hence, reflecting at ease in a rocking chair. The rabbit incident still lived on like a color photograph etched in mind. Yet the worries of the day were nowhere in the scene.

The ECK was saying: To be calm and happy, stay in a high state of spiritual consciousness. Then

*Whenever an out-of-the-ordinary event comes along to jolt our awareness, it pays to look again, and more closely.*

all will be well.

A healer of physical ailments once wrote a book. Emboldened by its large sales, he aimed later books at healing the mind and emotions. I remarked to my wife, "His next book will see him a spiritual leader."

Soon after, to keep a salivating publisher at bay, and to pay bills, there followed a tome on God.

Certainly, anyone may publish his theories about God. One man's God is another man's devil. After all, didn't Rebazar Tarzs say, "There is no mystery in God except that It is what each Soul believes that It is"?

It was expected, then, to read a blurb praising the wisdom in the author's latest offering. The blurb said that God changes as man's consciousness changes.

God changes?

Maybe the copywriter was trying to use a clever wordplay to attract public attention—to increase sales. No problem. Yet if the author, a self-proclaimed spiritual leader, had actually made that point, with a lot of dressing to fill up the book, I'd yawn and look elsewhere for truth.

The ECK writings, in contrast, cut through the murk like a laser. Many questions of a pure spiritual nature find a solution in the Shariyat, to the delight of a true seeker.

The everlasting scriptures of ECK teach in all sorts of ways. As seen above, they may illumine us through a waking dream. In another case, their wisdom may help us cut through the fog in a

*Many questions of a pure spiritual nature find a solution in the Shariyat, to the delight of a true seeker.*

copywriter's mind in regard to, say, God's unchanging nature. Beyond that are daily crises that tear us limb from limb over a matter of weeks, while we cry for a resolution.

In such an instance, life patches up our broken lives and transforms us into a more glorious vessel, to better receive God's healing, unfailing love.

A dear couple recently hit the wall. One of those life-changing episodes, a dark night of Soul, rocked the vessel of the family's comfort.

They'd come out survivors from a two-year tumult of gut-wrenching changes made to their satisfactory, yet wanting lives. Conditions were nothing to write home about then, but much better spiritually than in the years prior to that first rocking of stability.

This second rocking of their comfort zone stole up like a pickpocket. (That's usually the case with change, isn't it? Like a big joke gone sour.)

The couple's apartment lease was terminated with no warning, and without a reason. It caught them cash poor. The area's booming economy had blasted the cost of housing far beyond their means. Still, a replacement home had to be an easy commute to work.

Thus began a frantic search for new living quarters. Weeks of fruitless looking seemed like months in a thirsty land.

Out of the blue, when hopes and dreams had all but died, the ECK settled them into a much nicer place. Admittedly a small house with a shabby lawn, yet the interior was modern and attractive. A perfect find.

*In such an instance, life patches up our broken lives and transforms us into a more glorious vessel, to better receive God's healing, unfailing love.*

Halfway into house hunting, the woman said, "I've been reborn. I'm not the same person anymore."

His beaten response: "I'm exhausted; I have no idea how this is going to turn out. But I feel OK, stronger. I don't know why."

When the rocking of the family's ship closed another chapter, he summed it up. "So, a good ECK story of how Spirit came to help in a couple of ways."

It always does. So take heart and know that I am always with you.

*Take heart and know I am always with you.*

# 20

# What Kind of Experience Leads to God?

$\not\Join$

*O*nce as a youth I had a revelation of sorts. It was with surprise one day that a realization settled in. Not a gem of an eternal sort, you can rest assured, but it made me raise my eyebrows a bit in wonder.

"You and your body are a laboratory to gain knowledge," came the realization.

*Why did it take so long to figure that one out?* I mused.

The problem now, what to do about it? What was the smart thing to do? Like so many youth and adults, I did any number of things that a kindly observer could only term "random." In the end, no method of application came to mind, so I put this bit of realization in a safe place in the back of my mind in case a use should present itself one day. Then I jumped back into my usual habits.

"Life" consisted of doing things expected of me, along with a healthy dose of things that I wished to do. This led to a mixed life of good judgment in a sprinkling of things, but an excess of random acts.

*"You and your body are a laboratory to gain knowledge," came the realization.*

To be sure, Soul was collecting a basketful of rich experience. Yet to what end?

Experience was all it was. In a spiritual sense, you'd have thought this kid was on track. The purpose of life, after all, is to gather up as many rich experiences as possible, isn't it? All right, then, I was off and running.

But why the unrest? That was hard to say.

If experience itself is the measure of all things, then why is there so much unhappiness? Name one person without any experience.

Look at the compulsive gambler. He gambles a lot. And if he's had any rays of luck at all, he must have landed a few pots of gold in his time and used them to finance things he wanted to do. Yet he drinks, carouses, and gambles evermore, as if driven by a demon.

Scratch him, however, and underneath hides a most unhappy man.

Or take an employee in some organization for a number of years. He sports a reputation as a complainer. The company provides a living wage as well as health and other benefits, yet he's always grumbling about someone or something. Some think him a rebel; others, a fool. It takes all kinds to make up this world.

*Experience, to be sure, is the basis of knowledge. But is it enough for experience to lack a plan, purpose, or pattern?*

Experience, to be sure, is the basis of knowledge. But is it enough for experience to lack a plan, purpose, or pattern?

Let's say, it's OK for the first leg of the journey to God. However, the behavior that leads to such experience is of an unconscious sort. It's a bit like a budding herbalist who ventures into a field to gather a bunch of green plants. He knows, in general, plants are good.

But you and I know that just gathering an armful of green things and tossing them into a pot could produce a soup with an unhealthy surprise. Why, it could make the novice quite ill should his bundle contain some attractive sprigs of hemlock. They do bear a familial likeness to carrot tops.

You can see in a minute that this individual would be smart to exercise a bit of judgment while foraging in the fields.

Cows, for example, won't touch certain plants. Same with pigs and chickens. Whether for taste or health, they leave certain green things alone. Still, even animals make errors.

The point is that the simple gathering of experience has spiritual limitations. It's possible to get experience by falling out of bed, but of what use is it?

So experience itself is not the end of all things good. An ECK chela knows there's got to be more, because a life full of experience that adds up to more of the same, with unhappiness on top of it, is a tight circle. It goes nowhere. It comes to an end where it began, a rather useless exercise to keep on for all time.

Now we're looking at a spiritual seeker.

The seeker, like you once, has this feeling that life must have more to offer. He wants some of that undefined fulfillment too. Where to look, whom to ask?

Well, so it goes. The Mahanta, the Living ECK Master soon arranges things so the seeker may begin to find truth.

*The Mahanta, the Living ECK Master soon arranges things so the seeker may begin to find truth.*

That stage of unfoldment lies in your past. Unconscious experience, a lot of it, once brought you to ECK. After that humble beginning, however, didn't you notice that your experiences saw a change? Dreams, for example, began to take on order and meaning. Events in your daily life, too, seemed to suggest an underlying purpose as you began the Spiritual Exercises of ECK.

So, unconscious experience gave way to the *conscious* sort. Something was going on. It was like the hand of God come to give its blessings during your struggles with body, mind, and emotions.

To travel the second and most important part of your journey to the heart of your Creator demands both experience and *experiment*. Soul begins to make some experiments, with a purpose and pattern to them. Yet it takes a method. You guessed it, this method is rooted in the Spiritual Exercises of ECK. Simple though they be, they reveal one's determination to break free of the circle of karma that has kept him in spiritual slavery, lo these many lifetimes.

Experience is not sufficient unto itself. The search for God requires a higher set of experiences. The method to succeed in this longtime search requires an engine—your dear friends, the Spiritual Exercises of ECK.

There is a divine power in the charged words that come to you during the ECK initiations. A number of initiations nest within each of the major initiations, and all require diligence in contemplation if an individual hopes to unfold to the divine secrets that lie hidden in his heart.

*A number of initiations nest within each of the major initiations, and all require diligence in contemplation if an individual hopes to unfold to the divine secrets that lie hidden in his heart.*

Yes, there is a reason for doing the Spiritual Exercises of ECK on a daily basis. A lover of God must explore new ways to see and do the things of Divine Spirit, the ECK.

So go, see, and do in the right way, the ECK way.

*So go, see, and do in the ECK way.*

# 21

# The Golden Ring of Truth

*The love of SUGMAD (God) is so broad and deep that mankind can only see a few threads of ITS divine cloth.

That has the ring of truth.

Soul's relationship with Its Maker is beclouded. People see value where there is none, and nothing of substance when they have the good fortune to catch a glimpse of the Eternal. This beclouding of reality marks every aspect of living. It colors the values of individuals. Illusion—the inability of humanity to see a thing in a clear, consistent manner—accounts for the suspicion and evil on earth.

Illusion is seeing reality in the wrong way. It lacks the ring of truth.

Illusion makes for separation. People stand apart from their fellows, their equals in spirit, because of distinctions of station in life, color of skin, beliefs, and power. Differences raise fears.

And where does the notion of differences come from? It comes from the masses of people whose vision of their Maker is beclouded by their own frailties.

*Illusion is seeing reality in the wrong way. It lacks the ring of truth.*

They stand in their own way. And in the inimitable fashion of mankind, they persecute all the things they hate about themselves. So they direct their self-loathing at others. From a position above, like from a space station that circles the earth, an observer may look down upon a world dressed in blues, greens, and muted browns. A seemingly tranquil place.

However, earth is a cauldron. It is forever at the boiling point and must be watched with care lest it boil over.

And there are human organizations who work under the guidance of higher spiritual beings to tend the pot. So life on earth simmers along as it has ever since the dawn of mankind.

*Now, this earth is the cooking pot in which Soul at some point awakens.*

Now, this earth is the cooking pot in which Soul at some point awakens. It awakens a bit bewildered. In fact, It was bewildered during most of Its long sojourn on earth, eking out an uncertain existence in lifetime after lifetime. Each time It returned, It yawned and stretched. But each return proved to be a false awakening.

Soul, with memory wiped clean, was ready to begin each life anew. It was like spring. And then Soul trudged on to have thousands more of such experiences. But they were, at the heart, tired replays of those experiences in past lives.

Those ages of lifetimes were hardly lost or wasted. Soul was practicing to make perfect.

Besides, without a memory of having run the same course of experiences so many times before, It seldom got bored with the routine of it all.

Then one day, in one special lifetime, that all changed.

A spacewalker high above the earth, looking down, might have noticed a bright light, like a star, below. However, it would have taken the eye of Soul to see it.

That light, one of the few bright points upon the earth's surface, represented the birth of an individual who'd run the course the required number of times. This fortunate one's destiny would turn upon a chance to grab at the golden ring on the merry-go-round. When the ring came around, he was to stretch out and make a grab for it. Missed? No problem. The merry-go-round would go around again to offer another chance.

What is the golden ring?

It is the ring of truth.

The individual with his spiritual light turned up high is our old friend, the seeker.

His whole life's mission was The Search. For years, the fact that he was searching for some unrealized thing was hidden by duty to family, friends, society, and even to the little self (the sleeping human consciousness).

But his spiritual awakening did come. It was his destiny. Time and circumstances set the moment.

The pressures of life gathered to swamp him on the eve of his awakening. The seeker cried out for deliverance. He begged to be free of the self-made prison around him. Where was the golden ring of truth? When would the merry-go-round present it to him?

*The individual with his spiritual light turned up high is our old friend, the seeker.*

At that point the Master appeared.

Of course, his appearance did not assure a successful first try for the ring. That was up to the rider. The rider's fear kept him from stretching out far enough to reach it. Would he topple from his mechanical steed? Well then, perhaps the best course was not to stretch too far.

Yet the golden ring sparkled. The light of love streamed from it, and the rider desired it above all else. He knew it then. So during the next round he put aside the fear of falling and reached far. He caught at the ring, the golden ring, and had it.

The merry-go-round could stop. And so it did.

He dismounted, carrying his prize with him. Why, it was a magical thing. The owner of the golden ring of truth discovered a vast improvement in his vision. He could see better, farther. Everything shone with a new brightness.

And so the seeker now saw the Master, who'd been on the carousel all along, like a caring parent, to ensure a safe ride.

The circular ride on the carousel of reincarnation was over, and the real journey of life began. Soul's next destination was Its true home, the high worlds of God. Life took on meaning. The golden ring of truth gave Soul a new set of values, a sense of what is enduring and what is fleeting. It put Its attention upon the Eternal.

Tolstoy, the Russian novelist, philosopher, and mystic, once said, "The highest wisdom has but one science—the science of the whole—the science explaining the whole creation and man's place in it."

It has the ring of truth, doesn't it?

*The Shariyat-Ki-Sugmad*, Book Two, says this: "To the ECKist there is nothing more than the whole man."

It adds that an ECKist learns to get along on less food and leisure time, because of the time he spends in contemplation and the Spiritual Exercises of ECK.

"But most of all," it says, "he is mainly concerned with being himself and living, which means that he has learned to live with himself through self-discipline. He is responsible to himself and works toward a happiness which becomes a part of the whole of himself. In other words, he is integrated and is now a part of the universe instead of being only a part of his community, nation, and race."

You have obtained the golden ring of truth. Please help others have a chance at it too. For your efforts, I thank you.

*You have obtained the golden ring of truth. Please help others have a chance at it too.*

Acres and acres of diamonds glitter all around you. Look for the sparkles. Those are from seekers. Lead them to the Light and Sound of God.

## Chapter Seven

# Living in Service to All Life

# 22

# How the Holy Spirit Helps You

✷

    Some excellent ECK (Holy Spirit) Vahana (missionary) stories come to us from Sharmaine of Temple Services in Chanhassen. Names are changed, of course, for privacy.

These stories are like those you hear in whatever part of the world you live. So they are yours too.

Megan hadn't kept the Master's presence, especially during the Friday fast. This Friday would be different; she'd keep it all day. It was also her first day as a volunteer at a nursing home, where she was feeding an Alzheimer's patient. The patient was babbling. He wasn't making sense at all.

Suddenly, his words came into focus. He said, "Who's that man across the table from you, all in blue?"

You know it was the Inner Master, the Mahanta. Blue clothing are his signature. Megan was on track.

\* \* \*

Who of us hasn't been disturbed by a telemarketer during the dinner hour? Here's how

*Suddenly, his words came into focus. He said, "Who's that man across the table from you, all in blue?"*

Anne handles them:

A telemarketer wanted to sign her up for a newspaper, but she said she had access to it at work. She quickly added that she gets inner guidance in a grocery-store checkout line on what article to scan while waiting. In a library, she knows which journal to peruse. The caller got very excited.

"That happens to me too," he exclaimed.

So Anne told him about ECKANKAR and invited him to the ECK Worldwide Seminar. It was a graceful and natural opening. She stepped right in.

And telemarketers with credit-card offers hear this:

Anne says that her religion teaches her to be financially responsible, so she has no need for more credit cards. This piques their interest. A frequent response is, "What's your religion?"

"ECKANKAR, Religion of the Light and Sound of God." And the conversation goes on from there. She tells them how to get more information on ECK by visiting www.Eckankar.org on the Internet or by calling 1-800-LOVE-GOD.

Anne sees the pearls lying at her feet among the stones.

What about phone companies who pitch their services? She informs them she's happy with her current phone company, to which they usually reply, "In the future, if you ever become interested in our services you can call . . ." Anne, in turn, is ready with information on where they can learn more about the ECK teachings.

*Anne told a telemarketer about ECKANKAR and invited him to the ECK Worldwide Seminar. It was a graceful and natural opening. She stepped right in.*

She's alert to these openings laid out by the Master.

* * *

Andre, too, is an ECK Vahana. He and his wife live in the country in a woods, and recently a couple built a new home near their property. Andre and his wife invited them over for dinner. The new neighbor told of growing up in a Minnesota community, which had no lakes close by, so he wasn't exposed to ice hockey. But now he's just started watching the game and finds he knows all about it.

He said, "I know I was involved with hockey in other lifetimes."

Andre was amazed to hear his new country neighbor say such a thing, but he recognized the opening to tell of ECK.

At their next meeting, Andre said, "This might be of interest to you—in regard to hockey." Then he handed him a copy of *Past Lives, Dreams, and Soul Travel*.

His neighbor looked skeptically at the book. "I don't know what I think about this."

"What do you mean?" his wife chimed in. "You're talking about this stuff all the time." May the ECK bless our mates for being there when we need them but are too proud to admit it.

Notice, again, how nicely the Mahanta shows you what to do. Keep an eye out.

* * *

Juan saw a chance to tell a seeker about ECK through his profession. He is a bilingual inter-

*He said, "I know I was involved with hockey in other lifetimes." Andre was amazed to hear his new country neighbor say such a thing, but he recognized the opening to tell of ECK.*

preter in medical situations. One day a teacher brought a ten-year-old student to the hospital where Juan works.

"What brought you to Minnesota?" the teacher asked.

"My church, ECKANKAR."

"Is it Christian?"

"No," he said, "we have a living teacher."

Then, like the professional he is, he went back to interpreting. The situation gave no further opportunity for conversation. He'd wanted to offer her a HU card.

So that was that for then.

The teacher later found a way to reach him. Would he be willing to work with the patient when he returned to school? Juan was unable to give her an answer at the moment. But she called later to say the position wouldn't be available after all. Almost as an afterthought, she said, "But by the way, you mentioned something when we talked at the hospital."

Juan knew this was the true purpose of her call.

"Yes, you mean ECKANKAR?"

"Can you tell me more about it?" she asked.

So he faxed her an invitation to the state ECK regional seminar. She came for an hour. Past lives and reincarnation were among the subjects that really lit up for her. She had many questions. Later he told her of an ECK intro on reincarnation at a St. Paul library, but he didn't have all the details, like time and date.

A couple of weeks later, Juan was at the library

to check the location and poster for the event. And who should walk into the library but the teacher. She knew this was no coincidence. So Juan was happy. He could fill her in on the event, plus offer her a personal invitation with one of the posters.

Juan says, "Spirit opens up these little windows in the course of a day. People are craving to know what we have to share with them."

Yes, they are. The opportunities to tell others about ECK and Its wondrous ways are all around. Acres and acres of diamonds glitter all about you. Look for the sparkles. Those are from seekers. Lead them to the Light and Sound of God, which make their existence possible.

And if you would, please pass on to me in your monthly initiate report any of your singular successes. Thank you.

*The opportunities to tell others about ECK and Its wondrous ways are all around.*

# 23
# The Long Arm of the Mahanta

The Mahanta reaches out for seekers in surprising ways. A case in point is the story told by a Higher Initiate, whom we will call Mary, who is in Australia.

Mary has a friend, June (a pseudonym), who is an ECK initiate. June had been an initiate quite a few years, until about ten years ago, when she decided to step back from the outer works of ECK. She did so because she felt unworthy and unable to reach what she felt were the requirements needed as an initiate in ECK. Yet she kept up with the Spiritual Exercises of ECK and inner contact with the Master.

During this ten-year sabbatical from the outer ECK works, June decided to learn Mandarin Chinese. She is Chinese.

Fast-forward now to several years ago, when she came back to the outer ECK works and resumed the ECK Satsang classes. One day Mary called her. Would June like to give a short talk at the ECK Worship Service on how it was when she left the outer study and how it is now? June readily agreed.

*The Mahanta reaches out for seekers in surprising ways.*

Later, when the service was over and most people were gone from the ECK center, a car pulled into a parking spot right out front. An Asian man climbed out and then stood looking in at the ECK-center door.

"Would you like to come in and look around?" Mary asked.

Mary had a feeling that he had a hard time understanding English, so she called June over. June addressed him in Mandarin. Soon they were engaged in a lively conversation.

Later, June told Mary and other ECK initiates his story.

The man had never heard of ECKANKAR before. He was on a short vacation from Taiwan and had been looking for the marketplace. He had only stopped in front of the ECK center because he was looking for a parking spot. The only open one was right at the center's front door.

"This is a miracle!" he kept saying. "A miracle!" For the ECK and the Mahanta were exactly what he was looking for.

That is an excellent example of how the Mahanta's long arm reaches out to a true seeker. But then, likely as not, he calls on you to do your part. The path of ECK is one of giving and receiving, for that is the way of sure spiritual unfoldment. June undoubtedly learned this firsthand.

A few people among a thousand are ready for the ECK teachings of spiritual freedom. I have mentioned this in my talks and writings from time to time.

Jim, who lives in the northwestern part of the

*"This is a miracle!" he kept saying. "A miracle!" For the ECK and the Mahanta were exactly what he was looking for.*

U.S., did the math for his city of around a million people. He reasoned that since the Master had said "a few," he meant at least three, or he would have said "a couple of."

"A few people" in this case meant three thousand Souls ready to learn about the Mahanta and the ECK teachings. So Jim and other chelas made plans to find them.

In connection with these plans, Jim had a dream in which he was in the back of a church hall. Smoke began pouring into the room. Quickly, he opened the back door and found it led outside through a long hallway. Jim faced a choice: to save himself or go back into the room and look for trapped people.

He chose the latter. A door in front of him did not feel hot, so he opened it and began to coax people to leave by the back door. Many did.

What did Jim see as the meaning of his dream?

*I wonder if this is a metaphor for Dream 3000* (the name of the Vahana plans that he and others had drafted), he mused. *Perhaps,* he thought, *I will rescue those who find the formal religions suffocating.*

The long arm of the Mahanta.

The Mahanta works in many and diverse ways to reach out to people of all ages, including the youth.

Jack is an ECK initiate in South Africa. At the time he reported the following incident, he was working as a journalist for an investigative magazine.

He also ran a small project since 1996 that has taken a number of street children off the streets

*"A few people" in this case meant three thousand Souls ready to learn about the Mahanta and the ECK teachings. So Jim and other chelas made plans to find them.*

and put them into what he called "long-term upliftment." Some six years later, one of his youths landed in prison. The police had trumped-up evidence against him for possessing tools used for housebreaking—four spark-plug pieces.

It is necessary to mention here that all the youths in Jack's rescue-and-upliftment program knew about the Mahanta and the power of HU.

The accused youth sang HU in prison when someone wanted to fight him, when the prison guards threatened to beat him, and when he was lonely.

Finally, after numerous delays, his trial took place. The magistrate threw out the trumped-up police evidence and set him free.

That is another example of the Mahanta's long arm. Noteworthy is the fact that this ECK youth was a light of hope and guidance for other prison youths, speaking to them of higher principles in ways they could understand.

You, like him, can be an instrument for the Mahanta too.

*You, like him, can be an instrument for the Mahanta too.*

# 24
# Meetings with Two ECK Masters

It is always a pleasure to tell you about people who have met an ECK Master and how that contact raised their level of spiritual consciousness. Each story embodies a lesson. Whatever lesson each of you gleans from it may be worlds away from the insights of another chela.

So strap on your wings, and let's see where you fly!

In the first instance, "Andy" tells how he found ECKANKAR a few short years ago, and the way it changed him. He had lived and worked in New York City for many years. Then 9/11 struck. A short while later, a second shock: he arrived at his workplace to find the doors padlocked. Out of business!

Jobs were scarce; his savings ran out. Unable to pay rent, he was evicted from his apartment and lived in a homeless shelter. It was during these dark days that he found ECKANKAR.

One night, Andy had a vivid dream. A stranger motioned to him, with a gentle wave of the hand, to follow him to paradise. Andy reports that this

*One night, Andy had a vivid dream. A stranger motioned to him, with a gentle wave of the hand, to follow him to paradise.*

meeting ignited a fireball in his stomach. Only a few days hence, he found a flyer on a bulletin board announcing an ECKANKAR event. ECKists there gave him a very warm welcome. He knew he was home; he had found what he had been searching for.

The very next evening, Andy was off to the ECK center. The ECKists welcomed him with open arms. They invited him to view the videos and browse the library.

A surprise awaited him. On a wall hung a picture of the man who had called to him in that dream. It was Fubbi Quantz! Most afternoons that summer, Andy saw himself visiting the ECK center.

He says, "Although I found myself to be destitute for the first time in my life, I felt like the wealthiest man on earth!"

Paradise had found him, he continues. The Living ECK Master had found him, and he had found himself. And so, Andy became a member of ECKANKAR. That was another big change. The next one put him on his feet financially again: he moved to Chicago. There, a job opened up. His ECKANKAR membership materials, along with his first discourse, soon came in the mail.

Andy considers his new chela membership card to be his official birth certificate. And so it is.

*Andy considers his new chela membership card to be his official birth certificate. And so it is.*

\* \* \*

Now we will take a case from a side of service in ECKANKAR. Andy told us of his early days, when he first made contact with the teachings of Light and Sound. (Since then, he has begun to serve too. As a seeker, he was served. Now he serves others.)

"Mel" is on the other end of the spectrum, in terms of service. He is a RESA.

Shortly before he received news of his appointment, Mel, like Andy, had a vivid dream. He had, in this dream, gone to visit friends in a small town of 1,200. A town so small, he found it hard to believe he had actually lost his car. Curiosity intact, he began to explore the streets. He came upon a Middle Eastern bazaar.

The place was teeming with shoppers, whom colorful vendors tried to attract with both everyday and exotic items.

Mel continued his explorations. Soon his feet carried him to a large, spacious building, the noise of the bazaar faded in the distance. A bald man came out of the building. "I am so glad you are here," he said. "Come in, and I will show you what you can do to help."

Yaubl Sacabi, for that was indeed Mel's host, showed him two very large, round, etched-bronze pieces of art.

In the first was the figure of a man, arms and legs stretched out, a man detached from the world he lived in—Self-Realization. The second piece of art revealed a man standing quietly in the worlds of God, ready and willing to serve as the ECK's will was to be done.

This was God-Realization!

Mel recognized that these two precise etchings showed so well the two main goals of every ECK chela.

*The second piece of art revealed a man standing quietly in the worlds of God, ready and willing to serve as the ECK's will was to be done. This was God-Realization!*

Yaubl said, "Would you deliver them for me?"

As Mel was en route to make the delivery, he pondered the fact that everything done in behalf of the ECK Masters was a sacred act.

A man at the appointed place invited him in. Inside, on a table, stood a bronze sculpture of a man bound to confused and seemingly unconnected events. This man was clearly struggling. He was desperate to be free from that which bound him.

"There is more," he said, "but I don't know how to find the next step."

Mel then handed him Yaubl Sacabi's two gifts. The man was deeply touched. Mel left, but looking back, he saw the other looking at his "answers."

There are several important lessons in this story too. I am sure you will catch them.

*Mel pondered the fact that everything done in behalf of the ECK Masters was a sacred act.*

A Soul's final polishing may include the lowly art of cleaning windows. Indeed, everything is a miracle.

## Chapter Eight

# Creating a Life of Love and Beauty

# 25
# A Window-Washing Miracle

The physicist Albert Einstein once observed: "There are only two ways to live your life. One is as though nothing is a miracle. The other is as though everything is a miracle."

Perhaps it's fair to say that the difference between the two extremes is experience.

My whole life, I've had a desire to learn something new, because I felt that learning would make me ever more self-sufficient and happy. So late one Saturday morning when I was fourteen and at a church school away from home, a few of us students took a bus to the suburbs. A member of a local parish wanted us to clean the windows of his large home.

He provided two buckets of soapy water, two squeegees, and clean rags; pointed us in the direction of the windows; and vanished into his home to catch a ball game.

Left to our own devices, we set to with enthusiasm and good cheer. We had plans for the money. It would go toward fudge at the bakery on Sunday morning during our return to campus after services at a neighborhood church.

*Albert Einstein once observed: "There are only two ways to live your life. One is as though nothing is a miracle. The other is as though everything is a miracle."*

It was late autumn. The air had the first chill of winter's breath upon it. We worked like little demons to clean the windows, so we could escape to the dorm and warmth.

The ball game ended just as we'd completed the job. His team had lost.

Disgruntled by the loss, the homeowner came out into the increasing cold of late afternoon. A look at the first window produced a cry of distress. "It's full of streaks. I can't look at that all winter!" He set us to work to clean it again. But the rags kept leaving streaks on the pane, even when he tried to show us the right way to do it. Apparently, the rags still had soapsuds in them from the washing machine.

So his team had lost the game, and he had dirty windows to boot. Evening's shadows stole closer.

*The homeowner ran to check all the windows we'd labored over. "You'll have to do them all again," he said.*

He ran to check all the windows we'd labored over, then rushed back to our little shivering and now hungry knot of misery.

"You'll have to do them all again," he said.

It was obvious he'd have to help if his windows were to be spick-and-span by nightfall. He disappeared into the garage. A moment later he emerged with an armful of old newspapers.

"Now look here," he said. He picked up a sponge, washed a window, squeegeed it, then wiped it completely dry with a crumpled newspaper.

The window sparkled.

He ran off into the garage again and returned with another bucket and squeegee. Now there were three sets of cleaning equipment. Like the seasoned manager of a ball team, he divided us into three groups, with him leading one of them.

Then we all set out with a passion to reclean the windows. By day's end, there was just sufficient light to inspect and approve our mutual efforts.

So he got clean windows; we, hard-earned money for Sunday sweets. Both parties grew.

That day we, boys and homeowner alike, gained a bit in practical experience. Need I say, *conscious* experience? Even today, whenever I clean a window or a mirror, memories from that frosty autumn day still linger, to haunt and bemuse.

Spiritual experience can rise from a lesson of seeming insignificance like that. Imagine, then, the power of thousands of other minor, yet not so trifling, experiences which have accrued in this and past lifetimes.

Truth, the eternal sort, arises from a host of varied episodes. They've sharpened our understanding of divine love.

Yes, it may appear to be a stretch from a boy learning a better way to clean windows to gaining knowledge that, in the end, leads to eternal truth. But consider: What does truth require of a seeker? He must be able to see himself somewhat as he is, in both human and spiritual terms. A human does make mistakes. Yet Soul, the spiritual self, seeks to find the Eternal in spite of all human frailty.

Let's switch our focus for a minute.

A successful space ad by Joe Karbo that used

*What does truth require of a seeker? He must be able to see himself somewhat as he is, in both human and spiritual terms.*

to appear in magazines appealed to the secret laziness of many readers. The title read: "The Lazy Man's Way to Riches." A subhead added to the ad's power, giving it a one-two punch. It said: "Most People Are Too Busy Earning a Living to Make Any Money." This ad is among the best-selling ads of all time.

In a way, it promised a reader he could gain wealth with little or no effort. Yet, if he'd had a chance to observe Joe Karbo, he'd have discovered a quick-witted and creative genius at work. Notice: "at work."

Karbo knew human nature all too well and built his prosperity and success upon that knowledge.

Material success is but one of many steps a seeker may encounter on the path to God. Wealth, however, is neither here nor there. A spiritually advanced person may be either rich or poor in material goods. But whatever the condition, it's of his choosing. He's the sum of his own choices.

That is to say, he is to accept all responsibility for his station in life. Socrates, the great philosopher of early Greece, was a poor man. His family did not enjoy the comforts that could have been theirs, because Socrates found the choice of poverty more in accord with his mission to enlighten people. (Small wonder, then, that history suggests he was a henpecked husband.)

So what qualities does the Living ECK Master look for in a chela (spiritual student)?

Here are a few:

• accepts responsibility for his actions (does

*A spiritually advanced person is to accept all responsibility for his station in life.*

not blame society for them)
- knows the difference between right and wrong
- does not envy others at a higher station in life, etc.

Still, the Mahanta, the Living ECK Master points to the gulf between political and spiritual freedom. Those he chooses for disciples must, however, have the basics of natural law, an innate knowledge of divine law. Conscious experience will, via the Spiritual Exercises of ECK, bring a respect for its eternal principles, which lead to love and truth of the highest order.

A Soul's final polishing may include the lowly art of cleaning windows. Indeed, everything is a miracle.

*Conscious experience will, via the Spiritual Exercises of ECK, lead to love and truth of the highest order.*

## 26

# No Security Here, but Where?

How many times do you feel left to your own devices? What do you do then?

"Quiet minds cannot be perplexed or frightened," author Robert Louis Stevenson once observed, "but go on in fortune or misfortune at their own private pace, like a clock during a thunderstorm."

Let's take this idea to a higher level still. See what *The Shariyat-Ki-Sugmad* offers in this line of thinking:

"A specific attitude and viewpoint is necessary for the satisfactory utilization of the spiritual powers; he who uses them must be free from emotional bias and entirely detached and serene in his attitude. Otherwise he will be a failure at traveling the path to God."

Paul Harvey, the most listened-to radio newscaster in America for years, has much of such an attitude. It is undoubtedly the reason for his good health and longevity.

Beginning in March 2000, the stock market crashed. The perceived wealth of millions of

*How many times do you feel left to your own devices? What do you do then?*

investors was at risk. They saw the paper value of their retirement investments drop like a stone from a cliff. But the market rallied. People relaxed. Their material security looked sound again. The market's precipitous drop was only a "bad hair" month.

At the vanguard of this optimism rode Paul Harvey.

Every time the stock market rebounded from a new low, Mr. Harvey was on the radio with a note of encouragement during his daily news program.

"Only the jumpers get hurt," he counseled.

He was comparing the ups and downs of the market to a Ferris wheel. The market, he believed, was still on its way to the top and had merely paused to allow new riders to climb aboard. And when it reached the top, he further assumed, its descent would be as orderly and predictable as its rise had appeared to a money-hungry public.

Of course, the market proved his undue optimism in the wrong. It went down, ever down. But Mr. Harvey never lost his faith in a brighter tomorrow.

Meanwhile, many in his listening audience had lost most of their retirement investments.

Three years after the initial market crash, government reports began to show an increasing number of bright spots among so many dark ones in the economy. Our dear Paul Harvey, ever hopeful, gently chided his listeners for not climbing back on the stock-market Ferris wheel. The amusement ride was empty. There were plenty of seats available.

After three years of gloom and loss, however,

---

*The market proved his undue optimism in the wrong. It went down, ever down. But Mr. Harvey never lost his faith in a brighter tomorrow.*

Americans were afraid to get back on such a rocky ride of promised wealth and security.

People were sick and tired of the stock-market bubble. Instead, they switched their money to a new bubble: real estate. Prices for homes screamed upward and homes, even second homes, now appeared to be the place to get rich quick.

But, in time, all bubbles do burst.

What then? Where is the material security?

And so mankind's quest for material security lurches onward, picking up more believers for a ride to nowhere, but in a new area of risk.

Yet the point is about Paul Harvey's attitude. In lean times or fat, he always looks to the bright side of things. Even when he lost his voice. Such an affliction would be a disaster of immense proportion to a man whose radio career spanned decades. Every day his voice rasped more. One day, another news broadcaster sat in for him. Then, another and another. Finally, a team of them covered for him.

Mr. Harvey, meanwhile, sat at home, unable to speak. His voice had forsaken him, and its loss cut him off from his weekday visits with listeners.

Even his optimism finally bowed. There were times, he once confessed, that he wanted to—and perhaps, did—feel sorry for himself. But a lifetime of looking on the sunny side of life keeps a spark aglow in the heart. He never gave up hope. Somewhere, he instinctively knew, someone could restore his voice.

His broadcast studio was in Chicago. About a year later, he learned of an eminent voice specialist right there in the city who might help him.

*A lifetime of looking on the sunny side of life keeps a spark aglow in the heart.*

It turned out to be his dream come true. A simple office procedure removed an obstruction near his vocal cords and gave promise of returning his beautiful, resonant voice to the airwaves.

Months of recuperation followed. There were a number of disheartening setbacks on the road to a full recovery, but Mr. Harvey never lost faith. In time, his listeners were delighted to be reunited with an old friend. And as always, he was there to acknowledge the dark side of man's inhumanity to man in his news programs. But he balanced that with the positive things people of good heart can and do accomplish.

Let's lend an ear to the poet Henry Wadsworth Longfellow, too, on the right attitude:

"Look not mournfully into the past," he said. "It comes not back again. Wisely improve the present. It is thine. Go forth to meet the shadowy future, without fear."

Louis L'Amour, the stellar writer of Western stories, put it more succinctly:

"Few of us ever live in the present," he observed. "We are forever anticipating what is to come or remembering what has gone."

*So where should a Higher Initiate of ECK position himself amid the uncertainties of material security?*

So where should a Higher Initiate of ECK position himself amid the uncertainties of material security? Where else but with the Mahanta, the Living ECK Master? The Master shows the nearest door to heaven. All that's asked of the initiate is to keep his faith and love fixed on the Imperishable, the SUGMAD (God). The Mahanta is the true guide home. Do the Spiritual Exercises of ECK he gives you. They provide security beyond the reach of earth's sword.

Love God above all things. Love the ECK (Holy Spirit). Love the Mahanta, the Living ECK Master. Nurture and cherish your loved ones.

Remember, love yourself. You are Soul, a light of God.

Mr. Harvey, you may be sure, lets faith and love guide his every step. Let the Mahanta guide yours.

*The Spiritual Exercises of ECK provide security beyond the reach of earth's sword.*

# 27

# Gratitude Shows You Can Love

✦

*T*here are two topics I'd like to address in this letter to you.

First, briefly, a curious phenomenon in the spiritual works, the Spotlight of ECK (Holy Spirit). What is that?

When someone is under consideration for more responsibility, the ECK brings out all the bugs under his rug. It reveals his true state of consciousness. By word or deed he shows whether or not he is ready for the new position. You may, in time, learn the art of recognizing the Spotlight of ECK too.

The second topic involves gratitude.

It is one's response to the greatest gift there is—life itself.

When you hit the wall, you get a new appreciation for living. "Thank you for this gift of life," you say to the Mahanta (Inner Master). "I am so happy!" People who haven't had your experiences would have no idea what you're talking about. So we don't share much. The only way to understand is to go through a similar experience.

*The Spotlight of ECK (Holy Spirit). What is that?*

So we come to live more in silence about the secret things than we'd planned to do. Because before we have our life-changing experience, we can't know.

I constantly scan for subjects to talk about. There is such a broad field to draw on.

To begin, I open myself completely to the ECK to see what needs to be said. This may be for a meeting of ECKANKAR's Board of Trustees, seminar talk, publication like the *H.I. Letter*, or for my other writings. I do the research through the outer ways and means. Then I open myself to the SUGMAD (God) and to the ECK to see the images of what needs to be said.

Next, I need to translate those images into today's language. That's why much of my writing is simple. It leaves less room for misinterpreting and makes translating into other languages easier.

I take care to translate the images from the ECK to human language as accurately as possible. They flow through directly, in a burst.

Many are sharing their ideas from the mental arena, and it uplifts people. I look at the ideas and thoughts of philosophers. One thing that strikes me about Immanuel Kant was something he said that acts out an appreciation for life, which shows gratitude in expression.

He said, no ifs, ands, or buts.

By that he meant, make your statements clean and clear. Suppose one, for example, says to a student, "Study hard if you want to make your degree." Kant says, forget the stuff at the end. Say just, "Study hard."

---

*One thing Immanuel Kant said shows gratitude in expression. He said, no ifs, ands, or buts.*

When someone says but, it's a nail in the coffin of invention. A constant stream of contradictions shuts off creativity and a gift that may be offered.

And when someone says but, he's stopped listening.

So be aware when using *if*. And especially when using *but*, because it's limiting.

Move straight ahead. Don't clutter things with *if*, *and*, or *but*. It throws a condition under your feet that is a trip wire.

This is pretty much for ourselves, because in dealing with others, you may need to use *if*, *and*, or *but*. *And* is better because it doesn't limit and is a building block.

Yet, if someone's trying to make plans for *you*, then you may need to say, "But I don't want to." They have no right to make *your* plans.

On the subject of gratitude, never overlook those who are closest to you. Your family and those around you are number one to be grateful for. Once you can love those, it shows you have the capacity to love. Then you can love the Mahanta, the ECK, and the SUGMAD.

*Your family and those around you are number one to be grateful for.*

# 28
# It's a Good Life

*Ellen* is someone who passed through the mills of the gods and was ground exceedingly fine. (All names are changed in this article for privacy.)

Over eighty now, she can look back on a dynamic and event-filled life. It's not been an easy one. But amid the many days of fear, sorrow, and pain, there were times a rainbow would appear to remind her of the sunshine.

She'd grown up in a third generation of actors, but due to being an illegitimate child, she was often on her own, running scared.

At sixteen, Ellen took a job as an entertainer-dancer. She was booked for two weeks in a small upstate New York town. But when the owners saw her artless dancing, they put her out on the road, at midnight, with just train fare home. She was petrified. Alone and abandoned in a hard, merciless world, what could she do?

A man came along and offered to walk her to the railroad station. She had no choice. But she kept a two-foot distance from him.

At the station, he bought her ticket and told her to wait in the ladies' room all night, since there were no trains till morning.

*Alone and abandoned in a hard, merciless world, what could she do?*

*Not until she came into ECK years later did Ellen realize he was the ECK Master Paul Twitchell.*

Not until she came into ECK years later did Ellen realize he was the ECK Master Paul Twitchell.

Her life's been anything but a bed of roses. There've been so many ups and downs in her life before and after ECK that you don't want to hear about it. But a rainbow would appear unexpectedly in the worst of times.

Overall, it's been a good life.

Cathy, an ECKist from the midwestern U.S., would say the same thing. She'd had surgery to repair some damaged vertebrae, but the severe pain continued. The fourth doctor she consulted said it was time to get an MRI. It showed swelling and two or three broken vertebrae. Then began a round of painful biopsies with local doctors to find whether the swelling was from an infection or cancer.

Those biopsies seemed to go nowhere but to more painful biopsies.

Her next stop was a big hospital in Chicago. They took another biopsy under anesthesia. It showed there'd been a healing: it was scar tissue from a burned-out infection. There was no sign of cancer. The doctors needed only to repair all the damage. (In a dream, during the procedure, she'd been with the Mahanta.)

Her surgery was to last six hours; instead, it ran fourteen. A doctor told her he had nicked the iliac vein. She ended up getting seven pints of blood.

A neighbor, a surgeon, when told about it, blurted out that a cut iliac vein usually meant death.

During the surgery, Cathy had a near-death experience in which the Mahanta appeared to her in a brightly lit room. There she enjoyed the company of friends and family, including artist friends who'd "died." The Mahanta sometimes took her from the room into a dark area. Each time, she awoke in the intensive-care unit to the sound of a blood-pressure alarm. But each time, Cathy would leave again and awaken in the light.

The last time, the emergency alarm rang before she got all the way back. She laughed.

Pointing to the dark, she waved and told the Mahanta, "I'd better take care of this. I'll see you later!"

In other words, she realized, it was just as the teachings of ECK said. The Mahanta is there to escort you to the Light of God, to friends and family—and to joy.

And so she lost her fear of death, of pain, of being out of control, and of a lifelong fear of surgery.

They were all gone.

Cathy, too, would agree that it's a good life.

Jean, a drama therapist, was working in a psychiatric hospital with a group. People usually love a drama therapy session, for it helps open the door into a brighter place. But one particular day, nothing worked. A warm-up session that started promisingly soon fell flat. A game followed suit. Jean brought out the music and balls they often toss around to achieve group cohesion. That failed too.

She simply could not get into the flow of consciousness. The group just stared at her.

*She lost her fear of death, of pain, of being out of control, and of a lifelong fear of surgery. They were all gone. Cathy, too, would agree that it's a good life.*

Then Fred, a patient, asked permission to play his five-hundred-dollar violin for them. Jean cringed. Would this be another bust? But, OK, Fred could play. He was very proud of his instrument, so Jean asked him about the style of the violin, what was the resin, and how to tighten the bow. People were very interested in him and his instrument. He'd only been playing three years.

Fred put the bow up to his chin. "Here's a song you'll all recognize," he said. "If you don't, you are not alive!"

Then he began to play "Over the Rainbow." It was a most beautiful sound. Jean could barely hold back her tears in spite of missed notes. He was touching people deep in their hearts. It was a place filled with sadness and longing, for the quest to go home—the home of God. Afterward, Jean noted a change in the room.

Fred was a man whose life was one of isolation and distance. Today, though, he'd brought them all closer together.

He'd had something to give, and he had given it with all his heart. All were changed by it.

Jean might say, "It's a good life."

Someone once said that we're unhappy when we're only taking from others but happy when we're giving. Therein lies the secret of happiness. If you can take that idea with you, you'll be able to join Ellen, Cathy, and Jean and say, "It's a good life."

*Someone once said that we're unhappy when we're only taking from others but happy when we're giving. Therein lies the secret of happiness.*

An ECK initiation opens a gate to a new threshold. Mark this: the threshold of a place is but the entrance to a new level of spiritual possibilities.

## Chapter Nine

# A New Threshold of Love

# 29
# No Greater Love

The news media tell of dozens and dozens of those remarkable people who give of all they have to save the lives of others facing certain death. The highest stakes fall to the struggle for life over death.

Such giving may be of precious time or money, of organs, and above all, of one's own life.

What compels such sacrifice?

It is love.

Leigh Hunt, a poet, lived and wrote during the eighteenth and nineteenth centuries. A British citizen, he once spent two years in prison. His crime was having the audacity to criticize the prince regent. Hunt's prison visitors had among them some of England's finest and most celebrated poets: Byron, Moore, Lamb, and Shelley. They were all influential men.

However, none was as notable as a certain visitor to a dreamer in one of Hunt's poems, an oriental fable Hunt once wrote to express a simple truth about "no greater love."

Here is the story line of Hunt's poem:

Abou Ben Adhem awoke from a dream of

*What compels such sacrifice? It is love.*

peace. He'd awakened in his Astral body—though Hunt probably never knew of such a thing. Adhem was out of the body.

Moonlight streamed into the room, golden moonlight. In great wonderment he observed an angel writing in a book of gold. The angel's focus was all upon the book, and so he paid Adhem scant attention.

Adhem's curiosity stirred.

"What are you setting down in that great book?"

The angel glanced up, a look of divine rapture and sweetness radiating from his face.

"The names of those who love the Lord."

Eagerly Adhem asked, "And is my name one?"

"Nay, not so!" the angel said.

But Adhem's good cheer held fast. "Then write me as one who loves his fellowmen," he said. So the angel made due note of Adhem's name.

The next night Adhem was again awake in the Astral body. Again, the angel appeared in his bedroom, bathed in a wondrous golden light. The great book shimmered in the angel's hands. This time the angel opened the book to show the names of those whom a great love for God had blessed.

To his surprise, Adhem found that his name led all the rest.

\* \* \*

The ECK Masters, too, serve their missions due to a great, abiding love for their fellow men. Yet their love is equal for God and man alike. In fact, what sets them apart from man is their ability to

---

*The ECK Masters, too, serve their missions due to a great, abiding love for their fellow men. Yet their love is equal for God and man alike.*

love God back as much as God loves them. This, the majority of people do not have the ability to do.

And what great blessing, then, do the ECK Masters bring to those who would love God with all their heart and mind and being?

They bring the spark of love.

Like master outdoorsmen, the ECK Masters come upon the barely burning embers of a seeker's campfire.

Gently, with infinite love, the ECK Masters add a dry leaf to the embers, blowing ever so carefully. The ember flares. In turn, they add bits of the driest bark until the embers show a tiny flame. Next come fine shavings of dry wood. The flame gains in strength. Soon the embers are hot, flames eat greedily of branches, kindling, and finally, whole pieces of firewood and logs.

And so it is that a seeker's love for God comes to burn hot to return love to SUGMAD (God) too. All is in its rightful place.

*  *  *

The following story from *McGuffey's Fifth Eclectic Reader* illustrates how the ECK Masters go about raising the love and compassion of people.

A farmer from Maine was moving his family to Illinois during the 1800s. The journey was a long and hazardous one.

The family had journeyed no farther than New York when their only horse crashed through the rotten boards of a bridge over a fast-moving river. Both the horse and all their possessions were swept away in the torrent.

*Gently, with infinite love, the ECK Masters add a dry leaf to the embers, blowing ever so carefully.*

The man and his family were stranded. In a strange land, without goods or money, they faced ruin and starvation. There was no home to return to. Fellow travelers stopped to weigh the family's plight. Some were quick to blame the hapless farmer for trying to cross such a bridge with an overladen beast of burden. Still others showed great pity.

Then along the road came another traveler, an experienced man from out west. He surveyed the situation, then took out his wallet.

"All of you," he said, "seem to pity this unfortunate family. But how much?"

So saying, he put down a large sum of money and looked about him.

His act of ready generosity and his pointed question opened the eyes of the crowd. Needless to say, his example produced a magnificent bounty of charity, and soon there was more than enough money to buy another horse. The leftover funds were ample. The family could now complete the long journey to Illinois and settle there, able to fulfill every unexpected need.

It turned out that, in Illinois, the farmer's benefactor became his neighbor. Ever after, the grateful farmer was a friend indeed to a friend in need.

\* \* \*

This example shows the magnitude of the Masters' blessings too. They awaken a seeker's love for what he *can* see, his neighbor. In the end, his love may be so great as to love God as much as God loves him.

---

*The Masters' blessings awaken a seeker's love for what he can see. In the end, the seeker's love may be so great as to love God as much as God loves him.*

And keep the following in mind too:

When the Mahanta, the Living ECK Master suffers some illness, it is his choice. It demonstrates his love. It reflects the karma he's helping people and nations burn away. And so, the seekers among the masses will the sooner be purified. Then they're ready for the ECK teachings.

So love the Master. You do not have the strength to help carry his chosen burdens.

No greater love is our watchword.

*No greater love is our watchword.*

# 30
# What Gift Would You Give to the ECK Masters?

*S*omeone in a *Mystic World* class reported an eye-, ear-, and heart-opening question posed by the ECK Arahata.

The Arahata, however, began with another question. The topic up for discussion was the ECK Masters and gifts or blessings. The first question was an easy one. The Arahata said, "Has anyone received a gift or blessing from an ECK Master?"

Class members responded with a lot of enthusiasm. They told amazing stories of spiritual experiences, and there was little doubt they were doing the Spiritual Exercises of ECK.

Then came the second question: "Have you ever *given* a gift to an ECK Master?" It was a deeply thought-provoking one and caused the group to engage in serious reflection.

This was, indeed, the opposite side of the first question, which was about *receiving* divine gifts. The second was the other side of the coin. Yes, there were responses, but they were notably fewer than the first question had drawn.

*The Arahata said, "Have you ever given a gift to an ECK Master?"*

This chela took the second question home. He wondered what gift he could *give* to the ECK Masters. This inspired a spiritual exercise that he called "Gifts to the Masters." It is an easy and straightforward one. Just visualize, with love, a gift to each of several ECK Masters, a gift he might well appreciate.

Some of the gifts listed here are humorous. Yet all are inventive. They show that the ECK chela thought long and hard about his selections.

Keep in mind while reading on, what gifts you might give to someone who already seems to have everything.

*Fubbi Quantz.* This dear guardian of the ECK holy scriptures, the Shariyat-Ki-Sugmad, serves his mission at the Katsupari Monastery in northern Tibet, where they are kept on display. The chela's gift of love to him would be a hand-cleared trail up to the very top of the mountain. It, of course, is the site of the monastery.

*Lai Tsi.* He is the Chinese ECK Master who guards a portion of the Shariyat on Saguna Lok, the Etheric Plane. To him, the chela would give a wooden staff. He would carve on a knob in the wood an image of the Master's merry face. It would represent the time they sat in a forest in conversation, when unexpectedly, Lai Tsi rose and started up a mountain. He never looked back to see if the chela would follow. It was a test. (The chela did.)

*Yaubl Sacabi.* Luckily, the ECK Masters have a lively sense of humor. This Master would warrant two gifts. The first, a fireplace of hewn stone. It's to mark the time the chela saw his gleaming face in the fireplace at a lakeside resort in California. The second gift would be a soft alpaca cap with a blue star on top, to warm Yaubl Sacabi's head, which is completely bald, in the mountains.

*Gopal Das.* His work is largely on the Astral Plane, where he is guardian of the fourth section of the Shariyat. But he has a soft spot in his heart for the little children of ECK and the gentle of heart. The chela would present him with an extraordinary number of multicolored balloons. This would also include an air tank to fill them.

*Rebazar Tarzs.* This ECK Master often wanders the high, bleak heights of the Hindu Kush Mountains, on the border of Kashmir and in Afghanistan. He appears to many via Soul Travel, to help them become more godlike, more divine. Yet for all that, he spends days walking the rugged fastness of the Hindu Kush. The chela would present him with a pair of finely crafted sandals. They'd be woven of fine fibers, giving a warm and comfortable fit. They'd be durable too.

And when a seeker sees these sandals by the door of Rebazar's hut, he is filled with joy and a certainty of spirit. He knows he is about to receive the divine wisdom—and a cup of tea.

*Peddar Zaskq.* This ECK Master works tirelessly to open up the worlds of God to all humanity. So the gift to him would be an ancient and glorious book of maps, of all the worlds and spiritual geography.

*Wah Z.* The Mahanta, the inner side of the Outer Master, gets this little poem:

*And when a seeker sees these sandals by the door of Rebazar's hut, he is filled with joy and a certainty of spirit. He knows he is about to receive the divine wisdom.*

To Wah Z, I give my life.

I give my all, my heart, mind, body and
who I am as Soul.

Because he is the Mahanta, and
I am blessed
to be in his loving care.

*There you have it, a wonderful spiritual exercise.*

There you have it, a wonderful spiritual exercise. See what you can do with it. Your gifts are precious too.

# 31

# The Nature of the ECK Initiations

This letter is to clarify the nature of the ECK initiations.

Life, like the ocean waves, ebbs and flows. Sailors know the necessity of watching the tides at various hours of day or night. Ignorance could sink them.

An ECK initiation is one's entry into a greater realm of spirituality. Yet this entry is but to the threshold of that new level, and who may presume to be "confirmed in bliss"? Life ebbs and flows like ocean waters.

So an ECK initiation moves the initiate into the dimensions of a new beingness. But is he fixed in that state? Can he never slip and fall?

It happens all the time. It's life.

Soul in Its unfoldment, like the flowing tides of the great waters, goes forward. Yet there is a rest cycle too. One then either stands still or, in fact, slips backward to consolidate the recent advances in spiritual unfoldment.

Human nature is a reflection of Soul's ebbs and flows.

*Soul in Its unfoldment, like the flowing tides of the great waters, goes forward. Yet there is a rest cycle too.*

An ECK initiation, then, opens a gate to a new threshold. Mark this: the threshold of a place is but the entrance to a new level of spiritual possibilities. A new Fifth Initiate cannot claim the standing of one who is about ready to enter the Sixth Circle, though both are Fifths.

It is an unfortunate truth that people can and do fall from grace. An Eighth or Ninth Initiate is not confirmed in bliss by any means.

Consciousness, like life, ebbs and flows.

Listen to *The Shariyat-Ki-Sugmad*, Book One:

"Many are called to the path of ECK, but few are ever chosen to become the *true* [italics added] initiates of the nine worlds, and fewer still ever become eleventh-world initiates. The highway into the kingdom of heaven is narrow, and the way is strewn with the spiritual corpses of those who have failed. Only those who give up all for the love of the Mahanta can ever reach the gates of paradise."

That means, too, that an individual who has set foot upon the threshold of the Ninth Plane will either enter that house of God or turn and depart.

A First Initiate may visit the Soul Plane. However, a visit does not make him a resident with full privileges. An initiation in ECK is a foretaste of heaven.

Free will lets Soul unfold at Its own pace.

A loving father asked his two children to go to a well at some distance from home and fill a container of water. It happened that a high fence between two meadows ran to the well. Since the day was a pleasant one, the children were at lei-

---

*Free will lets Soul unfold at Its own pace.*

sure to go their own pace. One child went on one side of the fence; the second child, on the other.

All sorts of curiosities lay along the way. Rabbits and field mice hurried about their duties, while birds swept to and fro, collecting food for their young in nests. Ants built little fortresses. Butterflies put color into earth and sky. A lovely day.

Of course, the children reached the well at different times. And so also was their coming home.

How many times has the Living ECK Master seen a new initiate enter a higher spiritual world only to slide backward? A temporary slide, or a consolidation, is a natural event. It's in the fabric of being.

Yet should the individual take leave of the spiritual disciplines needed to remain at the new initiation, the spiral could take him down several ECK initiation levels.

Why this spiritual failure?

Here, listen to *The Shariyat-Ki-Sugmad*, Book Two:

"The reason for failure among so many who take the discourses of Eckankar and cannot practice Soul Travel, or the inner communication with another in the community of heaven, as this is called, is simply that they have no discipline. This discipline is important to everyone who belongs to the ECK colony. Those who practice their spiritual exercises, as laid down in the various discourses and written materials of ECK, will find results in some manner or form."

*The Shariyat* adds that the secret of ECK is not

*Yet should the individual take leave of the spiritual disciplines needed to remain at the new initiation, the spiral could take him down several ECK initiation levels.*

gained "by recitations, and austerities, and vows of silence."

How, then, is it gained?

"The secret of entrance into this holy community [the community of heaven] is through submission to the Mahanta, the Living ECK Master." So says *The Shariyat*.

*The vow implicit in the ECK initiation carries a great responsibility.*

The vow implicit in the ECK initiation carries a great responsibility.

Again, from the holy *Shariyat*:

"The whole thesis of the ECK chela's life is that he does in his own peculiar way what all ECKists are called upon to do; that their vows are a specific way of carrying out the initiation promises and that their community life is a particular manifestation of the life of the ECK, the body of the Mahanta of which they were made a member at the initiation of the First Circle."

People find ingenious ways to fool themselves. The reason is self-love instead of God love, because their actions lead toward the hope of self-gain in some material way.

An individual who claims to smoke simply to teach others about hypocrisy should take a close look at the hypocrite in his mirror. It's as Malcolm Forbes, the publisher, said, "Always listen to a man when he describes the faults of others. Most times, he's describing his own, revealing himself."

The smoker hasn't the discipline to break the smoking habit.

Understand, the Mahanta, the Living ECK Master gives freedom to all on the path of ECK. He will, however, need to act when allies of the

Kal (negative) power mislead the innocent.

People like to fool themselves; it bolsters their self-esteem. Vanity preens before the mirror, while humility sees its true self. Two faces, one mirror, two states of consciousness. Some drink alcohol because it's "good for the heart." So is purple grape juice.

How long will it take one to go to the well for the Water of Life and fetch it home?

Some kid themselves by a misapplication of talent on the Giani Marg, the order of Wisdom.

Read and heed: Live your vows in spirit and in truth.

Stephen Grellet, the French missionary, said, "I shall pass through this world but once. If, therefore, there be any kindness I can show, or any good thing I can do, let me do it now. Let me not defer it or neglect it, for I shall not pass this way again."

*Live your vows in spirit and in truth.*

# 32
# God's Searing Love

*You've* all heard of Rumi, the thirteenth-century Persian poet who was a secret follower of ECK. You've also heard of Shamus-i-Tabriz, the ECK Master, his teacher.

But what do you know of Rumi before he became a devotee of ECK? Let's take a look.

Rumi was born in 1207, in present-day Afghanistan. The dreaded Mongols were invading from the east, so his father uprooted the family and eventually settled in what is now Turkey. His father was a renowned teacher and preacher. He was a devout Muslim, well versed in Sufism too.

So Rumi grew up in educated circles, a student of his father. After his father's death, Rumi gained a reputation as a scholar and orator unmatched in the city of Konya.

And he was only in his twenties. But there was still more to come: the power of God's searing love.

By age thirty-seven, Rumi was a respected scholar but by no means a gifted poet. Then the power of divine love swept his old life clean. It came in the person of Shamus-i-Tabriz, and Rumi

*Then the power of divine love swept his old life clean. It came in the person of Shamus-i-Tabriz.*

was never again the same. (Shamus was sixty by then.)

Shamus met him in the marketplace, and this encounter threw Rumi into a daze. It vaulted him to a greater state of consciousness.

What mortal enjoyed such divine power as Shamus?

From that moment on, Rumi loved Shamus with all his heart and turned his back on his teaching duties. Instead, he began to listen to music and poetry, and dance to it. As you could expect, this netted him complaints from his disciples, who sorely missed the instruction of their highly popular teacher. Rumi ignored them.

His disciples' shock and outrage troubled him not in the least. He'd found his Master. Shamus he knew for a true messenger of the ECK (Holy Spirit), in Its twin aspects of God's Light and Sound.

Then, a calamity: Shamus had left Konya due to the jealousy and ill will of Rumi's disciples. It happened in the second year since the arrival of Shamus, and Rumi's world of sunshine went dark.

Rumi immediately sent a son to persuade Shamus to return to Konya. Shamus finally gave in, but he did so with strong misgivings. And the two were together for a few months more. Then, Shamus disappeared for good. Various reasons for his disappearance still make the rounds today. Yet no one really knows. A rather late legend has it that Rumi's disciples did him in. Other speculation claims he died in Iran, in 1273, at the ripe old age of eighty-nine.

*Rumi was never again the same. From that moment on, Rumi loved Shamus with all his heart.*

At any rate, there are said to be many tombs of his scattered all over the Islamic world.

After several years, Rumi resigned himself to a life without his beloved teacher and companion. He again lost himself in poetry, music, and dance. But how could he not miss the sun of his spiritual universe?

It was in the following years of loneliness and grief that a tremendous change occurred in Rumi. He developed into one of the most remarkable poets of the Persian language.

The power of love had transformed him.

So why had Shamus disappeared? There is little hard evidence to suggest his murder. Yet there is a clue. He saw his only purpose in coming to Konya as a special mission to help Rumi reach spiritual perfection. That and nothing more.

But Shamus was a hard teacher. The best way, he thought, to bring about spiritual perfection was to use separation from Rumi, the one whom he so dearly loved.

Rumi, he felt, needed "to be cooked" by separation. After all, his first departure had seen in Rumi a far greater devotion to God. Yet he still leaned too heavily on Shamus; it was holding him back spiritually, so Shamus may have decided to pop Rumi back into the oven.

A third reason that Shamus may have left Konya is that Shamus's job was done.

And so there we leave it. Yet we do know from our own experience in ECK that God's searing love can indeed make earth-shaking changes in our spiritual lives.

*We do know from our own experience in ECK that God's searing love can indeed make earth-shaking changes in our spiritual lives.*

# 33
# Closer to Finding God

*F*inding God is the sole purpose of your life. In a sense, it is like the old saying: "All roads lead to Rome."

But first you needed to learn the reason for that gnawing hunger inside you before coming to ECKANKAR. With tiny, sometimes trembling steps you made your way into an uncertain tomorrow.

Tomorrow always comes and then drifts on like a dream that never was.

Tomorrow bows before all the tomorrows to come. And they routinely appear until consumed by no-time, no-space, no-thing. All gone! Tomorrows are like spent booster rockets that have lifted their payloads into outer space, then fall away, unneeded. You eventually come to see tomorrows for what they are. They merely serve as doors, windows, or instruments to help you on your way to finding God.

So love the Mahanta. Trust him. For he is the Wayshower, the one who has been there, found God. He can choose the right roads, pick the best rest stops, and thus bring you to your destination by the most advantageous route.

*Finding God is the sole purpose of your life. So love the Mahanta. Trust him. For he is the Wayshower.*

Someone suggested that you would benefit by my June 2007 letter to the RESAs, so here it is:

Closer to finding God—that's what it's all about, isn't it? But how to get there?

"Elizabeth," a longtime High Initiate, knows the answer. She says, "In my spiritual life, I'm searching for even deeper answers—to life, to God—and then I find it all boils down to oneself. We become master of ourself, and it is all up to me. To living in the eternal moment, for it's all I have."

She recently had to endure the passing of her husband of sixty years. It was hard to do after so many years together, but it sharpened her focus on the reason for living.

Elizabeth wisely observes: "Learn to love more, serve the SUGMAD, love the Mahanta."

That is it in a nutshell!

Then, on the other end of the age spectrum, there is "David." He is another of those beloved by God. His youthful curiosity opens doors for him in the other worlds.

Once, he even met the famed ECK Master Rebazar Tarzs in the dream worlds.

David awoke on the inner planes. He was in a jungle, trying to survive and make his way to safety. He came to a bridge, and Rebazar Tarzs was seated beside it. On the other end of the bridge shone a pure white Light, so David boldly stepped onto the bridge to cross into the Light. Unfortunately, he began to sneeze. And then he became ill.

In the meantime, Rebazar simply sat there and

said, "You need to lose the fear!"

David awoke puzzled. More than anything else, he wanted to get closer to God. So for the next several days, he researched his ECK books on the five passions of the mind. He then realized the absolute need to control his mind. It will try to gain an upper hand over Soul as long as one is in the human body.

David therefore found himself at a crossroads familiar to everyone on the spiritual path. He longed to succeed spiritually. On the other hand, he was somewhat afraid to let go of his mind.

Any of you who have experienced Self-Realization know that Soul must gain control over the mind; otherwise there is no traveling into the higher worlds.

Is there a secret to this sometime conundrum?

There surely is. It's what Elizabeth said so simply: "Learn to love more, serve the SUGMAD, love the Mahanta."

A wonderful example of such single-minded love and service in order to gain mastery of herself, and thereby come closer to finding God, is that of "Carol." She had never owned her own home but wanted to. So she made a collage of the home she desired. It would even feature a Japanese garden with a fountain set into the ground, and goldfish.

Carol, a Second Initiate, knows that loving and trusting the Mahanta is a necessary first step to truly serving God.

So she fully trusted that the Mahanta would fulfill her dream, if it was to be.

Then she swung into action.

She began to look for houses, condos, and townhouses in her area. Carol was acting on a dream that had said it was time to look for a house to buy. Her faith is simply that "all things are possible with the Mahanta."

To make a long story short, she found her dream home. The Mahanta had come to her in dreams, telling her the reason not to buy the fourteen or so other homes she had considered, which included advice on financing too.

And incidentally, her new home came with a Japanese garden.

Closer to finding God! You will do well to keep this goal in the forefront as you go about your duties in serving life.

*Closer to finding God! Keep this goal in the forefront as you go about your duties in serving life.*

# Bibliography

**Chapter One: Walking Your Own Path to God**
1. *The H.I. Letter,* June 2006
2. _____, March 2001
3. _____, September 2003
4. _____, December 2001

**Chapter Two: Daily Spiritual Disciplines**
5. *The H.I. Letter,* March 2007
6. _____, June 2004
7. _____, June 2008

**Chapter Three: The Mahanta's Love for You**
8. *The H.I. Letter,* September 2002
9. _____, March 2002
10. _____, December 2007

**Chapter Four: How to Be a Better Vehicle for ECK**
11. *The H.I. Letter,* March 2006
12. _____, March 2003
13. _____, September 2000

**Chapter Five: Tests and Challenges of the Higher Initiate**
14. *The H.I. Letter,* June 2001
15. _____, March 2008
16. _____, December 2006
17. _____, September 2004

**Chapter Six: Overcoming Illusion**
18. *The H.I. Letter,* September 2005
19. _____, December 2000

20. _____, December 2002
21. _____, June 2002

### Chapter Seven: Living in Service to All Life
22. *The H.I. Letter,* December 2004
23. _____, June 2007
24. _____, September 2008

### Chapter Eight: Creating a Life of Love and Beauty
25. *The H.I. Letter,* June 2003
26. _____, December 2003
27. _____, December 2005
28. _____, March 2005

### Chapter Nine: A New Threshold of Love
29. *The H.I. Letter,* March 2004
30. _____, September 2006
31. _____, September 2001
32. _____, June 2005
33. _____, September 2007

# For Further Reading and Study

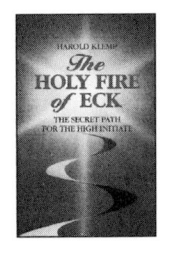

**The Holy Fire of ECK, Books 1 and 2**
Harold Klemp
The fire of God lights the way to personal spiritual growth and inspires service to all life.
*(For High Initiates only)*

**Riding for the ECK Brand**
Harold Klemp
In his talks to the H.I.'s, Sri Harold shares his message of love and commitment to the ECK.
*(For High Initiates only)*

**Wisdom from the Master on Spiritual Leadership: ECK Leader's Guide**
Also available: *Workbook for Wisdom from the Master on Spiritual Leadership*
Harold Klemp
The Mahanta, the Living ECK Master is every ECK leader's guide. Treasure his wisdom. Put it to use. It will help you serve as a loving vehicle for the Voice of God every day. There is no greater joy. *(For High Initiates only)*

**Ask the Master, Books 1 and 2**
Harold Klemp
Sri Harold addresses some of life's toughest questions. He offers compassionate, straight-to-the-point, and sometimes surprising answers.

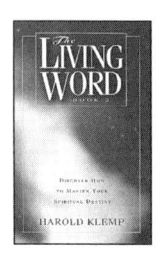

### The Living Word, Books 1, 2, and 3
Harold Klemp

The spiritual truth and divine love in Sri Harold's timeless articles from the *Mystic World* and *Eckankar Journal* show us how we can plan for and achieve tangible spiritual growth.

### Wisdom of the Heart, Books 1 and 2
Harold Klemp

Nearly two decades of Wisdom Notes, the letters from Sri Harold to the ECKists that appear in the *Mystic World*, teach new and practical ways to live your spiritual life to its fullest potential.

### The Shariyat-Ki-Sugmad,
Books One and Two

The "Way of the Eternal." These writings are the scriptures of ECKANKAR. They speak to you directly and come alive in your heart.

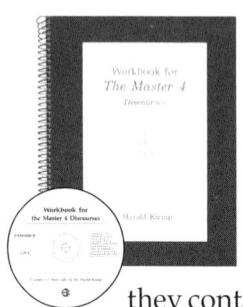

### Workbook for The Master 4 Discourses
Sri Harold Klemp

(For ECK members who have this discourse)

The exercises, activities, and excerpts in this workbook can help you become more aware of how the Mahanta works with you. Use this guided tour through the twelve discourse lessons to open your heart to the secret teachings they contain. Includes audio excerpts from Sri Harold (CD or audiocassette) that relate to each discourse lesson.

Contact ECKANKAR on availability of workbooks for other discourse series.

Available through ECKANKAR. Call (952) 380-2222 or write to ECKANKAR, Dept. BK70, PO Box 2000, Chanhassen, MN 55317-2000 USA.

# About the Author

Harold Klemp was born in Wisconsin and grew up on a small farm. He attended a two-room country schoolhouse before going to high school at a religious boarding school in Milwaukee, Wisconsin.

After preministerial college in Milwaukee and Fort Wayne, Indiana, he enlisted in the U.S. Air Force. There he trained as a language specialist at Indiana University and a radio intercept operator at Goodfellow AFB, Texas. Then followed a two-year stint in Japan where he first encountered Eckankar.

In October 1981, he became the spiritual leader of Eckankar, Religion of the Light and Sound of God. His full title is Sri Harold Klemp, the Mahanta, the Living ECK Master. As the Living ECK Master, Harold Klemp is responsible for the continued evolution of the Eckankar teachings.

His mission is to help people find their way back to God in this life. Harold Klemp travels to ECK seminars in North America, Europe, and the South Pacific. He has also visited Africa and many countries throughout the world, meeting with spiritual seekers and giving inspirational talks. There are many videocassettes and audiocassettes of his public talks available.

In his talks and writings, Harold Klemp's sense of humor and practical approach to spirituality have helped many people around the world find truth in their lives and greater inner freedom, wisdom, and love.

*International Who's Who of Intellectuals*
*Ninth Edition*

Reprinted with permission of Melrose Press Ltd., Cambridge, England, excerpted from *International Who's Who of Intellectuals, Ninth Edition,* Copyright 1992 by Melrose Press Ltd.